**Cultural And
Geographical
Exploration**

Race for the South Pole— The Antarctic Challenge

CHRONICLES FROM *NATIONAL GEOGRAPHIC*

Cultural And Geographical Exploration

Cultural And Geographical Exploration

Race for the South Pole— The Antarctic Challenge

CHRONICLES FROM *NATIONAL GEOGRAPHIC*

Arthur M. Schlesinger, jr.
Senior Consulting Editor

Fred L. Israel
General Editor

CHELSEA HOUSE PUBLISHERS

Philadelphia

CHELSEA HOUSE PUBLISHERS

Editor in Chief Stephen Reginald
Managing Editor James D. Gallagher
Production Manager Pamela Loos
Art Director Sara Davis
Director of Photography Judy L. Hasday
Senior Production Editor Lisa Chippendale

© 1999 by Chelsea House Publishers, a division of
Main Line Book Co. All rights reserved. Printed and
bound in the United States of America.

First Printing

1 3 5 7 9 8 6 4 2

19.95 4/99

Library of Congress Cataloging-in-Publication Data

Race for the South Pole: the Antarctic challenge: chronicles from
National Geographic / Arthur M. Schlesinger, Jr., senior consulting editor:
Fred L. Israel, general editor.
      p.   cm. — (Cultural and geographical exploration)
Includes bibliographical references and index.
Summary: Articles originally published in "National Geographic"
present the struggle of several nations to be the first to reach the
South Pole.
ISBN 0-7910-5100-5 (hardcover)
1. South Pole — Discovery and exploration — History — Juvenile
Literature.   2. Antarctica — Discovery and exploration — History —
Juvenile literature.   [1. South Pole — Discovery and exploration.
2. Antarctica — Discovery and exploration.]   I. Schlesinger, Arthur
Meier, 1917–   . II. Israel, Fred L.   III. National Geographic
Magazine.   IV. Series.
G863.R33   1999
919.8 — dc21   98-53262
                                          CIP
                                          AC

CONTENTS

Contents

"THE GREATEST EDUCATIONAL JOURNAL"

When the first *National Geographic* magazine appeared in October 1888, the United States totaled 38 states. Grover Cleveland was President. The nation's population hovered around 60 million. Great Britain's Queen Victoria also ruled as the Empress of India. William II became Kaiser of Germany that year. Tsar Alexander III ruled Russia and the Turkish Empire stretched from the Balkans to the tip of Arabia. To Westerners, the Far East was still a remote and mysterious land. Throughout the world, riding the back of an animal was the principle means of transportation. Unexplored and unmarked places dotted the global map.

On January 13, 1888, thirty-three men—scientists, cartographers, inventors, scholars, and explorers—met in Washington, D. C. They had accepted an invitation from Gardiner Greene Hubbard (1822-1897), the first president of the Bell Telephone Co. and a leader in the education of the deaf, to form the National Geographic Society "to increase and diffuse geographic knowledge." One of the assembled group noted that they were the "first explorers of the Grand Canyon and the Yellowstone, those who had carried the American flag farthest north, who had measured the altitude of our famous mountains, traced the windings of our coasts and rivers, determined the distribution of flora and fauna, enlightened us in the customs of the aborigines, and marked out the path of storm and flood." Nine months later, the first issue of *National Geographic* magazine was sent out to 165 charter members. Today, more than a century later, membership has grown to an astounding 11 million in more than 170 nations. Several times that number regularly read the monthly issues of the *National Geographic* magazine.

The first years were difficult ones for the new magazine. The earliest volumes seem dreadfully scientific and quite dull. The articles in Volume I, No. 1 set the tone—W. M Davis, "Geographic Methods in Geologic Investigation," followed by W. J. McGee, "The Classification of Geographic Forms by Genesis." Issues came out erratically—three in 1889, five in 1890, four in 1891; and two in 1895. In January 1896 "an illustrated monthly" was added to the title. The November issue that year contained a photograph of a half-naked Zulu bride and bridegroom in their wedding finery staring full face into the camera. But, a reader must have wondered what to make of the accompanying text: "These people . . . possess some excellent traits, but are horribly cruel when once they have smelled blood." In hopes of expanding circulation, the Board of Managers offered newsstand copies at \$.25 each and began to accept advertising. But the magazine essentially remained unchanged. Circulation only rose slightly.

In January 1898, shortly after Gardiner Greene Hubbard's death, his son-in-law Alexander Graham Bell (1847-1922) agreed to succeed him as the second president of the National Geographic Society. Bell invented the telephone in 1876 and, while pursuing his life long goal of improving the lot of the deaf, had turned his amazingly versatile mind to contemplating such varied problems as human flight, air conditioning, and popularizing geography. The society then had about 1100 members—the magazine was on the edge of bankruptcy. Bell did not want the job. He wrote in his diary though that he accepted leadership of the Society "in order to save it. Geography is a fascinating subject and it can be made interesting," he told the board of directors. Bell abandoned the unsuccessful attempt to increase circulation through newsstand sales. "Our journal," he wrote "should go to members, people who believe in our work and want to help." He understood that the lure for prospective members should be an association with a society that made it possible for the average person to share with kings and scientists the excitement of sending an expedition to a strange land or an explorer to an inaccessible region. This idea, more than any other, has been responsible for the growth of the National Geographic Society and for the popularity of the magazine. "I can well remember," recalled Bell in 1912, "how the idea was laughed at that we should ever reach a membership of ten thousand." That year it had soared to 107,000!

Bell attributed this phenomenal growth though to one man who had transformed the *National Geographic* magazine into "the greatest educational journal in the world"—Gilbert H. Grosvenor (1875-1966). Bell had hired the then 24-year-old Grosvenor in 1899 as the Society's first full-time employee "to put some life into the magazine." He personally escorted the new editor, who will become his son-in-law, to the Society's headquarters—a small rented room shared with the American Forestry Association on the fifth floor of a building, long since gone, across 15th street from the U. S. Treasury in downtown Washington. Grosvenor remembered the headquarters "littered with old magazines, newspapers, and a few record books and six enormous boxes crammed with *Geographics* returned by the newsstands." "No desk!" exclaimed Bell. "I'll send you mine." That afternoon, delivery men brought Grosvenor a large walnut rolltop and the new editor began to implement Bell's instructions—to transform the magazine from one of cold geographic fact "expressed in hieroglyphic terms which the layman could not understand into a vehicle for carrying the living, breathing, human-interest truth about this great world of ours to the people." And what did Bell consider appropriate "geographic subjects?" He replied: "The world and all that is in it is our theme."

Grosvenor shared Bell's vision of a great society and magazine which would disseminate geographic knowledge. "I thought of geography in terms of its Greek root: *geographia*—a description of the world," he later wrote. "It thus becomes the most catholic of subjects, universal in appeal, and embracing nations, people, plants, birds, fish. We would never lack interesting subjects." To attract readers, Grosvenor had to change the public attitude toward geography which he knew was regarded as "one of the dullest of all subjects, something to inflict upon schoolboys and avoid in later life." He wondered why certain books which relied heavily on geographic description remained popular—Charles Darwin's *Voyage of the Beagle*, Richard Dana, Jr.'s *Two Years Before the Mast* and even Herodotus' *History*. Why did readers for generations, and with Herodotus' travels, for twenty centuries return to these books? What did these volumes, which used so many geographic descriptions, have in common? What was the secret? According to Grosvenor, the answer was that "each was an accurate, eyewitness, firsthand account. Each contained simple straightforward writing—writing that sought to make pictures in the reader's mind."

Gilbert Grosvenor was editor of the *National Geographic* magazine for 55 years, from 1899 until 1954. Each of the 660 issues under his direction had been a highly readable geography textbook. He took Bell's vision and made it a reality. Acclaimed as "Mr. Geography," he discovered the earth anew for himself and for millions around the globe. He charted the dynamic course which the National Geographic Society and its magazine followed for more than half a century. In so doing, he forged an instrument for world education and understanding unique in this or any age. Under his direction, the *National Geographic* magazine grew from a few hundred copies—he recalled carrying them to the post office on his back—to more than five million at the time of his retirement as editor, enough for a stack 25 miles high.

This Chelsea House series celebrates Grosvenor's first twenty-five years as editor of the *National Geographic*. "The mind must see before it can believe," said Grosvenor. From the earliest days, he filled the magazine with photographs and established another Geographic principle—to portray people in their natural attire or lack of it. Within his own editorial committee, young Grosvenor encountered the prejudice that photographs had to be "scientific." Too often, this meant dullness. To Grosvenor, every picture and sentence had to be interesting to the layman. "How could you educate and inform if you lost your audience by boring your readers?" Grosvenor would ask his staff. He persisted and succeeded in making the *National Geographic* magazine reflect this fascinating world.

To the young-in-heart of every age there is magic in the name *National Geographic*. The very words conjure up enchanting images of faraway places, explorers and scientists, sparkling seas and dazzling mountain peaks, strange plants, animals, people, and customs. The small society founded in 1888 "for the increase and diffusion of geographic knowledge" grew, under the guidance of one man, to become a great force for knowledge and understanding. This achievement lies in the genius of Gilbert H. Grosvenor, the architect and master builder of the National Geographic Society and its magazine.

Fred L. Israel
The City College of the City University of New York

THE RACE FOR THE SOUTH POLE: AN OVERVIEW

FRED L. ISRAEL

The South Pole lies near the center of Antarctica at the point where all the earth's lines of longitude meet. At this point, there are six months of complete daylight and six months of complete darkness. While the North Pole is located in the Arctic Ocean, the South Pole is almost at the center of the Antarctic continent. Antarctica, with its ice cap, is larger in area than either Europe or Australia. It is isolated by the Atlantic, Pacific, and Indian oceans. Ships must navigate around icebergs and break through ice piles to reach it. The recorded temperature is the world's lowest—bitter winds prevail. Thick layers of ice and snow pressed together over millions of years bury most of the continent. Yet, this remote and desolate land has been the goal of explorers for more than two centuries.

In 1774, British captain James Cook, in an attempt to locate Antarctica, sailed further south than any European had ever gone. He circled Antarctica but the ice surrounding it prevented him from sighting land. The actual existence of the continent remained unproven until 1840.

Of the many voyages to Antarctica in the late 19th century, the most noteworthy was that of the HMS *Challenger* in 1872–76. This British vessel, the first steamship to cross the Antarctic Circle, carried out major oceanographic studies. Tens of thousands of photographs were taken. Perhaps the *Challenger*'s greatest contribution to the knowledge of Antarctica was its scientific confirmation that a continent really existed. This early period of exploration is a gripping saga of horrendous weather conditions, dangerous currents, and subfreezing temperatures that made these expeditions most dangerous and costly in human lives.

As the 19th century ended, efforts to reach Antarctica and the South Pole intensified. In 1895, Norwegian explorers made the first known landing on the Antarctic mainland, and between 1901 and 1904, Robert Scott and a team of British explorers became the first to do an inland exploration of the continent. Ernest Shackleton, a member of Scott's team, returned in 1907. Food shortages forced his group to turn back 97 miles from the South Pole, close enough to prove that the pole was on land rather than beneath a frozen sea. The race for the ultimate honor of being the first to reach the South Pole was on.

The *National Geographic* magazine closely followed the race to reach the pole. In 1901 alone, three major expeditions left for Antarctica. Geographers cabled the magazine with the latest information. In these pages, we learn about the German expedition (1901–3) which, after sighting the continent, was entrapped by ice. This expedition used balloons to survey the terrain and an Edison phonograph to record penguin noises for the first time. There was anxiety in the spring when blasting and sawing failed to set the ship free. The problem was solved by laying rubbish some 2000 feet to the open water. This dark area absorbed the heat of the sun and a channel was eventually melted. The *National Geographic* also printed a firsthand account of the 1901 Swedish expedition that ended when the ship was caught and crushed by ice. And the magazine covered the 1901–4 British expedition led by Robert Scott on his first expedition to Antarctica. Rarely have so many real life adventure stories appeared in one magazine.

The final race to the South Pole involved two fiercely competitive explorers who never met— Robert Scott (1868–1912) and Roald Amundsen (1872–1928). Scott led the British government and Royal Geographic Society's second expedition to the South Pole in 1910. From his camp on Ross Island, Scott started over the ice shelf with sleds in November 1911. He and his men reached the South Pole on January 17, 1912, but they found that Amundsen, a Norwegian explorer, had beaten them by one month and two days. Weary and disappointed, they began their return. Scott had relied on Siberian ponies to pull the sleds. But the ponies became exhausted and had to be shot. Without them, the men had to pull the sleds and carry the supplies. All five members of Scott's party died of cold and hunger. Their bodies with their records and diaries were found at their last campsite.

Roald Amundsen led the first expedition to reach the South Pole. Amundsen, an experienced Norwegian arctic explorer, had organized an expedition to the North Pole. When he learned that Robert E. Peary had already reached it, he changed plans and headed south. Amundsen and his men spent the Antarctic winter of 1911 at the edge of the Ross Ice Shelf. On October 19, 1911, after spring had arrived, they set off for the pole in four sleds pulled by 52 Eskimo dogs. Two months later, on December 14, measurements showed that they had reached the South Pole. After three days, they began the return trip, leaving behind a tent and a Norwegian flag. The route Amundsen had chosen was shorter than Scott's and covered flatter terrain. The dogs, unlike the Siberian ponies, withstood the hard work and cold.

The dramatic and moving race to reach the South Pole is one of the great epics of survival. It is chronicled here in the pages of the *National Geographic* magazine.

PLANS FOR REACHING
THE SOUTH POLE

By Gilbert H. Grosvenor

THE return of the *Belgica* in early spring, with the splendid record of being the first vessel to pass a winter within the Antarctic circle, and the bold landing of Captain Borchgrevink and his scientific staff on Victoria Land, where they are now making the first attempt ever made by man to winter on Antarctic land, have given great impetus to the projected Antarctic expeditions from England and Germany. Announcement is made that the British government is ready to grant a subsidy of $200,000 for the Antarctic expedition that is to set out in the summer of 1901 under the joint patronage of the Royal Society and of the Royal Geographical Society, and unless the promoters of the German expedition are being misled in their expectations, the Reichstag will soon guarantee substantial aid to the German National expedition. As one of the main subjects to be dealt with at the approaching International Geographical Congress at Berlin will be the mutual coöperation of these two expedi-

tions, it may not be inopportune to review briefly the plan and route of each.

It was originally intended by the Antarctic Committee, representing the Royal Society and the Royal Geographical Society, that the English expedition should consist of two ships, and that it should be under naval discipline and led by naval officers. In consequence, however, of the unwillingness of the government to consider such a plan with favor, the committee finally determined to equip but one vessel and to make an appeal for funds to the general public. The appeal has met with so generous a response that, including the splendid gift of $125,000 by Colonel Longstaff, $200,000 has been obtained. The plans of the expedition have not yet been finally determined in all their details, but it has been decided that the ship shall follow what is known as the South American route, sailing from the South Shetland islands southward to Alexandria Land. Here, at about 70° south by 90° west, a landing will be made, if practicable, and the first station established. Continuing onward, their course being dependent upon the amount of ice encountered, the party expect to establish on Cape Adare, Victoria Land, a second station, from which the great dash for the South Pole will be attempted, and in the vicinity of which the principal scientific work will be accomplished.

The movement for a distinctly German expedition to the South Pole may be said to date back to the early seventies, when Dr. Neumayer, the originator and organizer of the entire undertaking, began his agitation to that end. But his untiring advocacy of Antarctic research gained no practical recognition until 1895, when the Bremen meeting of the German Geographentage acknowledged its importance. Finally, somewhat over a year ago, plans took such definite shape that Dr. Erich von Drygalski, professor at the Imperial University of Berlin, was chosen as the leader of the expedition. Since then the route to be followed has been carefully determined, and nearly all the details for a two years' exploration have been arranged.

The principal danger to navigation in the Antarctic region is not ice pressure, for the currents radiate outward and not inward, but rather the stormy nature of the sea. Captain Drygalski proposes, therefore, to construct his ship on lines that will insure seaworthiness. This he believes can be secured by a vessel staunchly built of wood, with strong internal supports, which will at the same time afford protection against powerful magnetic influences.

The Kerguelen islands, lying in the Indian ocean at 70° east by 50° south and open to navigation at all seasons of the year, are to be the starting point. From these islands the route follows a line southwestward to some point on Wilkes Land, where a winter station will be built upon the edge of the ice-sheet and systematic observations taken. In the early spring an advance will be attempted on sleds across the ice in the direction of the magnetic pole, and in the fall a return will be made in a westerly direction along the little-known coast of Wilkes Land. Perhaps the party will be able to reach the most southerly known land, Victoria Land, discovered by Ross in 1842. As the English explorers are to build a station on the edge of this same Victoria Land and thence proceed southward as well as along Wilkes Land, Victoria Land will be the objective meeting ground of both expeditions. But naturally no geographic limits can be set in a region about which scarcely a single conclusion can be formed.

Captain Drygalski has repeatedly emphasized a condition now prevailing in southern waters which is especially noteworthy in view of the statement of Dr. Supan that we are now passing through an unusually warm-temperature period. This condition, as stated by him, is as follows: "The unusual quantity of drift-ice which first appeared in the South Atlantic ocean in 1891 and 1894, and then in the Indian ocean from 1894 to 1897, has each year advanced further toward the east and has now reached the Kerguelen islands, which are for the most part beyond the northern limit of drift-ice. From its nature we are able to determine that it is land-ice which has at last broken away after years of confinement to the mainland, a phenomenon well known as happening at long intervals in the northern parts of Greenland. Similar unusual variations in the conditions of the ice in the Antarctic region have been previously remarked. Though Captain Weddell, in 1823, from the South Orkney islands was able to advance unchecked as far as 74 degrees of latitude, and thence reported a sea free of ice as far as the eye could reach, all subsequent explorers have found an impenetrable barrier in front of them long before reaching that point." Inasmuch as a less obstructed advance than hitherto will be possible after the disappearance of this remarkable quantity of drift-ice, the next few years will be especially favorable for the resumption of Antarctic exploration.

Apart from purely scientific reasons, an ambition to advance German naval prestige is a prominent motive in the advocacy of a national expedition. The following paragraph, quoted from the *Kölnische Zeitung*, tends to show that the same logic that prompted the purchase of the Caroline and Mariana islands will be the most convincing argument for any vote by the Reichstag in favor of a large subsidy for the expedition: "For naval supremacy are necessary not only men-of-war and a merchant marine, but also an active participation in those scientific undertakings which lead to man's conquest of the sea. Such enterprises we Germans formerly left to others. Then we not only considered strategic points in distant seas unnecessary for ourselves, but actually surrendered to foreign hands, one after another, the approaches to our own harbors. Each course was equally inglorious; but about 1860 a desire arose for a personal share in the exploration of the North Polar regions, and from this feeling has grown the demand for a German fleet and the renewal of the plan for a canal to the North sea and of other similar projects. The honest conviction has come that all these enterprises are mutually dependent and but parts of one whole. To be strong at sea in the knowledge of readiness to fight, to be strong at sea in the consciousness of a peaceful commerce that carries our flag into every port, to be strong because of a scientific and intellectual conquest of the sea, are the rights of a great people working for one end— national development. Therefore let us hope that the German Antarctic expedition will not only add great honor to our scientists, but also bring new glory to German valor at sea."

The advantages, both from a geographic and general scientific point of view, of a further exploration of the South Polar regions have been so repeatedly set forth that it is hardly necessary to enlarge upon them here. Briefly they may be stated as: the verification or disproof of the existence of a vast Antarctic continent; the determination of the origin of the cold ocean currents which have their rise in the south; the study of the nature of ice itself, of the differences between land-ice, sea-ice, river-ice, etc; and the investigation of the conditions of atmospheric pressure and temperature, of volcanic action, and of terrestrial magnetism within the Antarctic circle.

WORK IN THE
ARCTIC AND ANTARCTIC

A Scottish expedition will undoubtedly be organized to coöperate with the English and German Antarctic expeditions of 1901. The Weddell sea quadrant, south of the Atlantic Ocean, will be the Scottish sphere. As previously noted in the NATIONAL GEOGRAPHIC MAGAZINE (vol. X, no. 8), the British sphere will be south of the Pacific Ocean and the German south of the Indian Ocean.

Lieutenant Robert E. Peary has probably by this time left his winter quarters at Cape Sabine, Ellesmere Land, and is well started on his dash for the North Pole. The series of caches of stores planted by him last year will lessen the difficulties of his advance to Cape Joseph Henry, where the real trouble will begin. Mr. Peary planned to take about a dozen picked Eskimo and some 80 dogs and as many loaded sledges as the latter can drag. When a sledge has been emptied it will be sent back to Cape Sabine with one of the drivers, and the rest will push on. Thus he hopes to reach Cape Joseph Henry with a large supply of provisions. From this point he will then set out with only two companions.

The first South Polar expedition to winter on Antarctic land has successfully reached Wellington, New Zealand. Mr. Borchgrevink, the leader of the party, reports that the south magnetic pole has been located, and that the expedition reached latitude 78° 50′, the farthest south ever attained by sledge. The expedition, which was fitted out by Sir George Newnes, of London, left Hobart, Tasmania, on December 19, 1898. During the latter part of February, 1899, the members landed from the *Southern Cross* near Cape Adare, Victoria Land, it having been arranged that the steamer should leave them there with a full equipment of every kind, and should return for them early in 1900. Mr. Borchgrevink's party consisted of nine, including himself. Lieut. W. Colbeck, R. N. R., was selected as first magnetic observer, to be assisted by Mr. Louis Barnacchi; Mr. N. Hansen and Mr. Hugh Evans were chosen as zoölogists, and Dr. H. Kloevstad as medical officer. With them went two natives of Finland to look after ninety dogs.

Another effort to discover some clue to the fate of Andrée will be made this summer. The

Swedish-Russian Expedition, which will leave about June 1 for Spitzbergen to relieve the party that is at present engaged in the work of measuring an arc of the meridian in that latitude, plans to make a detour to King Charles Land and carefully search the entire neighborhood. It will be remembered that in September of last year a buoy was picked up on the north coast of King Charles Land, at 80° north latitude and 25° east longitude, marked "Andrée's Polar Expedition." When taken to Stockholm and opened, it proved to be what Andrée had called "the North Pole Buoy," and in which he was to place a message when he passed the North Pole. However, a microscopical examination of the interior could discover no message. As the buoy could not have drifted to King Charles Land from the neighborhood of the Pole, the only conclusion possible is that it was a part of the wreckage of the expedition, and that possibly more wreckage may be found near by.

SOUTH POLAR EXPLORATION

THE arrangements for the British and German South Polar Expeditions which sail from Europe in August, 1901, are nearly completed. It is expected that the English boat, the *Discovery*, will be launched in March at Dundee. She is a good strong boat, built on different lines from the *Fram*, for the latter was planned to resist, or rather escape, tremendous ice-pressure, while the *Discovery* was modelled to withstand the attacks of a boisterous sea. The German boat, building at Kiel, is smaller and lighter than the *Discovery* and follows somewhat the lines of the *Fram*.

The two ships sail from Europe together. The official statement of their plan of co-operation is as follows:

"When they reach the far South they will separate with a carefully arranged plan of work for each. The Antarctic regions have been divided into four quadrants. First, the Victoria quadrant, which extends from 90 degrees east to 180 degrees, and includes Victoria Land; second, the Ross quadrant, from 180 degrees to 90 degrees west, south of the Pacific Ocean; third, the Weddell quadrant, from 90 degrees west to 0 degree (Greenwich meridian), the Weddell Sea; and fourth, the Enderby quadrant, from 0 degree to 90 degrees east, which includes Enderby Land. Two quadrants have been assigned for exploration and research to each expedition, the British taking the Victoria and Ross, and the German the Weddell and Enderby."

Both expeditions hope to be able to spend three years in the work. Captain Drygalski, the famed explorer of Greenland, leads the German party, while Captain Scott of the British Navy, young, hardy, and level-headed, directs the English.

WORK IN THE ANTARCTICS

PLANS are under way for five expeditions to southern regions, two of which—the English and the German—set out in July, in costly ships specially constructed for the purpose.

The *Discovery*, the first ship ever constructed in England for purely exploratory work, was recently launched on the Firth of Tay. The *Discovery*, which is the vessel of the **English Antarctic Expedition**, is the sixth of her name in the annals of British exploration. The first *Discovery* carried Hudson to Hudson Bay in 1610, on the ill-fated voyage when his crew mutinied and abandoned him in a tiny boat to perish on the great bay which he had discovered. The second of the name one hundred years later made a voyage to Hudson Bay. The third was the second ship in Cook's third voyage, in which he discovered the Hawaiian Islands, only to be murdered there a few months later. In the fourth Vancouver explored the Gulf of Georgia and the shores of the island which bears his name—1791–'95, and the fifth was the second ship of the Arctic expedition of Sir George Nares.

The present *Discovery* is as staunchly built as experience and science can make her. She is a combined sailing and steam vessel, with engines of 450-horse power, and will be able to steam about eight knots an hour. At the water line she is 170 feet in length, with an extreme breadth of 33 feet; her mean draft is 16 feet and her displacement 1,750 tons.

Captain Scott will have under him four other officers, two of them belonging to the navy and two to the Royal Naval Reserve. The second in command will be Lieutenant Armitage, whose three years' experience in Franz Josef Land with Jackson should be of immense service, especially if he is placed in command of a land party. There will be three civilian scientific specialists and two medical officers, both of them qualified to undertake certain departments of scientific work. The petty officers and crew will number about 25, so that the complete complement of the *Discovery* is not likely to exceed 40. There will be some 20 sledges and 20 dogs, some of the sledges being light enough to be easily drawn by men.

The *Gauss*, for the **German Antarctic Ex-**

pedition (named after the Göttingen professor who did so much to stimulate Antarctic research), was launched at Kiel early in April. The German ship, like the *Discovery*, is built mainly of wood, the only material which is elastic and strong enough to resist ice pressure and the boisterous seas of the south polar regions. She is some twenty feet shorter than the English vessel, but is broader, and her displacement is 300 tons less. The crew will consist, in addition to Dr. von Drygalski, of four scientific assistants, a captain, a first officer, two mates, an engineer, ten seamen, six assistant engineers and stokers, a cook, and a steward—28 in all. Each of the officers has a cabin to himself, while the crew have four large rooms. All the dwelling-rooms will be heated by steam, and it is calculated that a temperature of 50° Fahr. will be maintained within when that outside is as low as 22°. Electric light will be provided throughout practically the whole ship, and an acetylene apparatus may possibly also be installed. Laboratories and other special arrangements are provided for scientific work, while, as in the British ship, dredging and sounding apparatus have been provided. Dr. von Drygalski is planning to take 50 dogs. He, as well as the English captain, has included a balloon in the equipment.

A map showing the routes of the English and German expeditions was published in this Magazine, in No. 8, vol. x. The English expect to establish a station on Cape Adare, Victoria Land, which will be the base of their land parties, while the Germans plan to make their base on some point in Wilkes Land. Each vessel will carry sufficient stores for 3 years, as it is probable that each party will remain that time within the Antarctic Circle.

The **Swedish Antarctic Expedition**, under Dr. Otto Nordenskjold, has engaged the *Antarctic*, the vessel with which Dr. Nathorst made his notable explorations on the east coast of Greenland in 1899. This party may possibly leave in September, but the chances are that they will not set out until 1902.

Plans for the **Scottish Antarctic Expedition** are progressing. This expedition will probably not set out until the year 1902.

The **Duke of Abruzzi** is organizing a south polar expedition to start in June, 1902. He is enthusiastically supported by all Italians.

GEOGRAPHIC NOTE

The **German South Polar Expedition** will take a full equipment of aerial apparatus to make systematic kite ascensions from aboard ship during the voyage southward and also during the months in the Antarctic regions. The *Monthly Weather Review* states that the kites "are of three sizes: the large Marvin, like those used by the Weather Bureau, of 6⅓ square meters surface; Hargrave kites, of 4 and 2¾ square meters surface, and light Eddy kites, of 2¾ square meters, which are very advantageously used in lifting and sustaining the larger kites with instruments in light winds." Probably no expedition has ever made such complete preparation for the systematic exploration of the upper air conditions in South Polar regions.

THE BRITISH ANTARCTIC EXPEDITION

THE *Discovery*, carrying the British National Antarctic expedition, is now well on her way to South Polar regions. The proposed work of the party has been carefully outlined by the presidents of the Royal Society and of the Royal Geographical Society in their instructions to Captain Scott and to Dr. George Murray, the scientific director. The instructions to the commander are as follows:

1. The Royal Society and the Royal Geographical Society, with the assistance of His Majesty's Government, have fitted out an expedition for scientific discovery and exploration in the Antarctic regions, and have entrusted you with the command.

2. The objects of the expedition are: (*a*) to determine, as far as possible, the nature, condition, and extent of that portion of the South Polar lands which is included in the scope of your expedition, and (*b*) to make a magnetic survey in the southern regions to the south of the 40th parallel, and to carry on meteorological, oceanographic, geological, biological, and physical in-

vestigations and researches. Neither of these objects is to be sacrificed to the other.

3. The scientific work of the executive officers of the ship will be under your immediate control, and will include magnetic and meteorological observations, astronomical observations, surveying and charting, and sounding operations.

4. Associated with you, but under your command, there will be a civilian scientific staff, with a director at their head. A copy of his instructions accompanies these instructions to you.

5. In all questions connected with the scientific conduct of the expedition you will, as a matter of course, consider the director as your colleague, and on all these matters you will observe such consideration in respect to his wishes and suggestions as may be consistent with a due regard to the instructions under which you are acting, to the safe navigation of the ship, and to the comfort, health, discipline, and efficiency of all under your command. Those friendly relations and unreserved communications should

be maintained between you which will tend so materially to the success of an expedition from which so many important results are looked for.

6. As the scientific objects of the expedition are manifold, some of them will come under the immediate supervision of the director and his staff; others will depend for their success on the joint coöperation of the naval and civil elements, while some will demand the undivided attention of yourself and your officers. Upon the harmonious working and hearty coöperation of all must depend the result of the expedition as a whole.

7. The expedition will be supplied with a complete set of magnetic instruments, both for observations at sea and on shore. Instructions for their use have been drawn up by Captain Creak, R. N., and yourself and three of your officers have gone through a course of instruction at Deptford with Captain Creak and at Kew Observatory. The magnetic observatory on board the *Discovery* has been carefully constructed with a view to securing it from any proximity to steel or iron, and this has involved considerable expense and some sacrifice in other respects. We therefore impress upon you that the greatest importance is attached to the series of magnetic observations to be taken under your superintendence, and we desire that you will spare no pains to ensure their accuracy and continuity. The base station for your magnetic work will be at Melbourne or at Christchurch, in New Zealand. A secondary base station is to be established by you, if possible, in Victoria Land. You should endeavor to carry the magnetic survey from the Cape to your primary base station, south of the 40th parallel, and from the same station across the Pacific to the meridian of Greenwich. It is also desired that you should observe along the tracks of Ross, in order to as-

certain the magnetic changes that have taken place in the interval between the two voyages.

8. Geographical discovery and scientific exploration by sea and land should be conducted in two quadrants of the four into which the Antarctic regions are divided for convenience of reference, namely, the Victoria and Ross quadrants. It is desired that the extent of land should be ascertained by following the coast lines, that the depth and nature of the ice cap should be investigated, as well as the nature of the volcanic region, of the mountain ranges, and especially of any fossiliferous rocks.

9. A German expedition will start at the same time as the *Discovery*, and it is hoped that there will be cordial coöperation between the two expeditions as regards magnetic and meteorological observations, and in all other matters if opportunities offer for such coöperation. It is understood that the German expedition will establish an observatory on Kerguelen Island, and will then proceed to explore the Enderby quadrant, probably shaping a course south between the 70° E. and 80° E. meridians, with the object of wintering on the western side of Victoria Land, whence exploring sledge parties will be sent inland. The government of the Argentine Republic has undertaken to establish a magnetic observatory on Staten Island.

10. You will see that the meteorological observations are regularly taken every two hours, and, also, in accordance with a suggestion from the Berlin committee, every day at Greenwich noon. It is very desirable that there should, if possible, be a series of meteorological observations to the south of the 74th parallel.

11. As regards magnetic work and meteorological observations generally, you will follow the program arranged between the Ger-

man and British committees, with the terms of which you are acquainted.

12. Whenever it is possible, while at sea, deep-sea sounding should be taken with serial temperatures, and samples of sea water at various depths are to be obtained for physical and chemical analysis. Dredging operations are to be carried on as frequently as possible, and all opportunities are to be taken for making biological and geological collections.

13. Instructions will be supplied for the various scientific observations; and the officers of the expedition will be furnished with a manual, prepared and edited by Dr. George Murray, on similar lines and with the same objects as the scientific manuals supplied to the Arctic expedition of 1875.

14. On leaving this country you are to proceed to Melbourne, or Lyttelton (Christchurch), New Zealand, touching at any port or ports on the way that you may consider it necessary or desirable to visit for supplies or repairs. Before leaving your base station you will fill up with live stock, coal, and other necessaries, and you will leave the port with three years' provisions on board, and fully supplied for wintering and for sledge-traveling.

15. You are to proceed at once to the edge of the pack and to force your vessel through it to the open water to the south. The pack is supposed to be closer in December than it has been found to be later in the season. But this is believed to depend rather on its position than on the time, and the great difference between a steamer and a sailing vessel perhaps makes up for any difference in the condition of the pack.

16. On reaching the south water you are at liberty to devote to exploration the earlier portion of the navigable season; but such exploration should, if possible, include an examination of the coast from Cape Johnson to Cape Crozier, with a view to finding a safe and suitable place for the operations of landing in the event of your deciding that the ship shall not winter in the ice.

The chief points of geographical interest are as follows: To explore the Ice Barrier of Sir James Ross to its eastern extremity, to discover the land which was believed by Ross to flank the barrier to the eastward or to ascertain that it does not exist, and generally to endeavor to solve the very important physical and geographical questions connected with this remarkable ice formation.

17. Owing to our very imperfect knowledge of the conditions which prevail in the Antarctic seas, we cannot pronounce definitely whether it will be necessary for the ship to make her way out of the ice before the winter sets in or whether she should winter in the Antarctic regions. It is for you to decide on this important question after a careful examination of the local conditions.

18. If you should decide that the ship shall winter in the ice, the following instructions are to be observed:

a. Your efforts, as regards geographical exploration, should be directed, with the help of depots, to three objects, namely, an advance into the western mountains, an advance to the south, and the exploration of the volcanic region.

b. The director and his staff shall be allowed all facilities for the prosecution of their researches.

c. In carrying out *a* and *b* due regard is to be had to the safety and requirements of the expedition as a whole.

d. You have been provided by Sir Leopold McClintock and by Dr. Nansen with complete details respecting sledgework both by men and dogs, and you have yourself superintended every item of the preparations connected with food, clothing, and equipment. You will be guided by the information and knowledge thus acquired.

e. Lieutenant Armitage, R. N. R., who has been appointed second in command and navigator to the expedition, has had experience in the work of taking astronomical, magnetic, and meteorological observations during three Polar winters. He has also acquired experience in sledge-traveling and in the driving and management of dogs. You will, no doubt, find his knowledge and experience of great use.

f. Early in 1903 your ship should be free from the ice of the winter quarters, and you will devote to further exploration by sea so much of the navigable season as will certainly leave time for the ship to return to the north of the pack ice. Having recruited at your base station, you will then proceed with your magnetic survey across the Pacific and return to this country.

19. If, on the other hand, you should decide not to winter, you will bear in mind that it is most important to maintain scientific observations on land throughout the winter, and therefore if you are able, in consultation with the director, to find a suitable place for a landing party between Cape Johnson and Cape Crozier, and decide that such a party can be landed and left without undue risk, the following instructions will apply:

a. You will land a party under the command of such person as you may appoint. Such party shall include the director, the physicist, and one of the surgeons, and such other persons as you may consider desirable; but no person is to be left without his consent in writing, which you will be careful to obtain and preserve.

b. You will give every practicable assistance in establishing on land this party, which you will

supply with all available requisites, including a dwelling hut, an observer's hut, three years' provisions, stores, fuel, sledges, and dogs.

c. No landing party is to be established on any other part of the coast than that between Cape Johnson and Cape Crozier, as it is above all things essential that in case of accident the approximate position of the party should be known.

d. Before it is so late as to endanger the freedom of your ship, you will proceed north of the pack and carry out magnetic observations with sounding and dredging over as many degrees of longitude (and as far south) as possible, so long as the season and your coal permit, and then return to your base station, whence you will telegraph your arrival and await further instructions.

20. You are to do your best to let us have and to leave where you can statements of your intentions with regard to the places where you will deposit records, and the course you will adopt, as well as particulars of your arrangements for the possible need of retreat, so that in case of accident to the ship or detention we shall be able to use our best endeavors to carry out your wishes in this respect.

21. In an enterprise of this nature much must be left to the discretion and judgment of the commanding officer, and we fully confide in your combined energy and prudence for the successful issue of a voyage which will command the attention of all persons interested in navigation and science throughout the civilized world. At the same time, we desire you constantly to bear in mind our anxiety for the health, comfort, and safety of all entrusted to your care.

22. While employed on this service you are to take every opportunity of acquainting us with your progress and your requirements.

23. In the unfortunate event of any fatal accident happening to yourself or of your inability, from sickness or any other cause, to carry out these instructions, the command of the ship and of the expedition will devolve on Lieutenant Armitage, who is hereby directed to assume command and to execute such part of these instructions as have not been already carried out at the time of his assuming command. In the event of a similar accident to Lieutenant Armitage, the command is to devolve on the executive officer next in seniority on the articles, and so on in succession.

24. All collections and all logs (except the official log), journals, charts, drawings, photographs, observations, and scientific data will be the joint property of the two societies, to be disposed of as may be decided by them. Before the final return of the expedition you are to demand from the naval staff all such data, which are to be sealed up and delivered to the two presidents or dealt with as they may direct. The director of the civilian scientific staff will be similarly responsible for the journals, collections, etc., of the officers under his control. You and the other members of the expedition will not be at liberty without our consent to make any communication to the press on matters relating to the affairs of the expedition, nor to publish independent narratives until six months after the issue of the official narrative. All communications are to be made to us, addressed to the care of the secretary of the National Antarctic expedition, London.

25. The *Discovery* is not one of His Majesty's ships, but is registered under the Merchant Shipping Act, 1894, and is governed by it. Copies of this act will be supplied to you. You will see that the officers and crew sign the ship's articles as required by the act. The scientific staff will not sign articles, but are to be treated as cabin passengers. You must be careful not to take more than 12 persons as passengers.

26. The vessel has been covered by insurance, and, in the event of her sustaining any damage during the voyage, to recover the claim from the underwriters it will be necessary for you to call in the services of Lloyd's agent, or, in his absence, an independent surveyor, at the first port of call, in order that the damage may be surveyed before repairs are effected. His survey report, together with the accounts for repairs and supporting vouchers, should be sent to us by first mail, together with a certified extract from the official log reporting the casualty.

In the event of damage occurring after you have left civilized regions precise particulars should be entered in the log, and the damage should be surveyed and repaired as soon as you return to a port where Lloyd's agent or other surveyor is available.

27. The *Discovery* is the first ship that has ever been built expressly for scientific purposes in these kingdoms. It is an honor to receive the command of her; but we are impressed with the difficulty of the enterprise which has been entrusted to you and with the serious character of your responsibilities. The expedition is an undertaking of national importance, and science cannot fail to benefit from the efforts of those engaged in it. You may rely upon our support on all occasions, and we feel assured that all on board the *Discovery* will do their utmost to further the objects of the expedition.

INSTRUCTIONS
TO THE SCIENTIFIC DIRECTOR
OF THE CIVILIAN SCIENTIFIC STAFF

1. The Royal Society and the Royal Geographical Society have approved your appoint-

ment as director of the civilian scientific staff of their Antarctic expedition.

2. A copy of the instructions to the commander of the expedition accompanies these instructions, which are supplemental to them. You will see from the instructions to the commander what the objects of the expedition are, and your position relatively to them.

3. You will direct the scientific work of the gentlemen who have been appointed to assist you.

4. The names of the gentlemen associated with you are as follows: (1) Mr. Hodgson, biologist; (2) Mr. Shackleton, physicist. The services of the two medical officers will be at your disposal for scientific work when not engaged on the work of their own department, namely, Dr. Koettlitz, botanist, and Dr. Wilson, zoölogist.

5. You will note that the commander of the expedition has been instructed to communicate freely with you on all matters connected with the scientific objects of the expedition, and, as far as possible, to meet your views and wishes in connection with them. The societies feel assured that you will coöperate and act in concert with him, with a view, as far as possible, to secure the success of an enterprise which it is hoped will be attended with important results in the various branches of science which it is intended to investigate.

6. All collections, logs, journals, charts, drawings, photographs, observations, and scientific data will be the joint property of the two societies, to be disposed of as may be decided by them. Before the final return of the expedition you are to demand from the staff under your control all such data, which are to be sealed up and delivered to the two presidents or dealt with as they may direct. On the return of the expedition you will be expected to superintend the distribution of specimens to specialists approved of by the two councils or their representatives and to edit the resulting reports. You will also be expected to contribute a report on the scientific results of the expedition for the official narrative. As it may be desirable during the progress of the voyage that some new scientific discovery should be at once made known in the interest of science, you will in such a case inform us of it by the earliest opportunity.

7. You and the other members of the expedition will not be at liberty, without our consent, to make any communication to the press on matters relating in any way to the affairs of the expedition, nor to publish independent narratives until six months after the issue of the official narrative. All communications are to be made to us, addressed to the care of the secretary of the National Antarctic expedition, London.

8. Should any vacancies in the scientific staff occur after the expedition has sailed from England, you may, with the concurrence of the commander, make such arrangements as you think desirable to fill the same, should no one have been appointed from England.

9. You and the members of the scientific staff will be cabin passengers, joining the expedition at your own risk, and neither the owners nor the captain are to be responsible for any accident or misfortune which may happen to you. You will obtain from each member a letter to this effect.

The instructions are signed by the presidents of the Royal Society and the Royal Geographical Society.

THE GERMAN SOUTH POLAR EXPEDITION

By Dr. Georg Kollm, Editor and Secretary of the Geographical Society at Berlin

THE object of the German Antarctic expedition is the scientific exploration of the South Polar regions, particularly on its Indo-Atlantic side.

In pursuance of this object, it left Germany on the 11th of August, 1901, and is proceeding to Three Island Harbor, Royal Sound, in the Kerguelen Islands, where a base station will be established. In December, 1901, it is expected that the expedition will be ready for its real work of exploration and will push on toward the south as far as practicable. Should land be reached, a station will be founded and maintained for a year and the ship wintered there. Whether any later attempt to push still farther south will be made is not yet determined. It will not, at all events, be undertaken unless the conditions should prove particularly favorable.

The expedition has general orders to remain until its tasks are satisfactorily executed, but in any case not to remain beyond June, 1904, at which date it must report at some harbor in communication with home. Should no news be received of the expedition by the first of June of that year, it will be in order to consider the expediency of fitting out a relief ship.

The leader of the expedition, Dr. Erich von Drygalski, of Berlin, was appointed by His Majesty the Emperor, and has thoroughly studied the problems of South Polar regions. He has been placed in absolute control of the South Polar ship *Gauss*, its personnel and equipment. All the arrangements for the work to be carried on from the time the ship left Germany are under his direction and subject entirely to his control. Marine laws regulate the position of the ship's company toward its leader.

The expedition is an undertaking of the German Empire, and is fitted out through the Secretary of State for the Interior, Herr Dr.

Graf von Posadowsky-Wehner. It sails under the Imperial Service flag, and its officers and men bear special service designations authorized from the highest quarters. It is thoroughly well equipped, both scientifically and practically, for its ($10,000) mission. In addition to the funds provided by the Empire, about 40,000 marks in small amounts have been contributed by private societies. The interest aroused in the expedition throughout the Empire has been very great, and has led to the presentation of many valuable gifts and offerings which will add much to the efficiency of the equipment.

All the members of the expedition will be paid their regular and special remuneration from the imperial funds. They are also well insured against accidents and diseases caused by the climate. Risks too great for ordinary marine insurance companies to assume are borne by the Empire.

The results of the expedition and the collections made by it will be the property of the Empire, which will assume charge of their disposal. The scientific members of the expedition will be employed in the arrangement of the collections in such manner as their usefulness on the expedition warrants. They have to address all their suggestions and desires to the leader of the expedition, who will make all further arrangements.

The personnel of the expedition, beside the leader, who will conduct the oceanographical and geodetic work, are as follows

a. The scientific members: Prof. Dr. E. Vanhoffen, Kiel, for zoölogy and botany; Dr. H. Gazert, Munich, physician and bacteriologist; Dr. E. Philippi, Breslau, for geology and chemistry; Dr. F. Bidlingmaier, Lauffen, for earth-magnetism and meteorology.

b. The commander of the *Gauss*, a captain of the Hamburg-American line, Hans Ruser, from Hamburg, who was selected with the permission of His Majesty the Emperor.

c. The ship's officers: W. Lerche, from Stettin, first officer; R. Vahsel, from Hanover, second officer, both from the Hamburg-American line; L. Ott, from Hochst, second officer; A. Stehr, from Hamburg, first engineer.

d. The crew of the *Gauss*, which consists of two assistant engineers, two machinists, two boatmen, one Norwegian pilot, one cook, one steward, 6 seamen, and five stokers—in all, 20 men.

e. The personnel selected for the Kerguelen station consists of Dr. E. Werth, from Munster, as biologist; Dr. K. Luyken, from Munich, as meteorologist, and two seamen.

The Kerguelen station is chiefly intended for magnetic and meteorological observations, which, as well as similar work conducted by the German Chief expedition, will be carried on in accordance with the international program agreed on with England. This program has been sent to all States having magnetic-meteorological stations, as well as to the stations themselves, with the request for coöperation. Many have already signified their readiness to do so. It will also be followed at the station established by the Argentine Republic on Staten Island. Coöperation in all other sciences with the English expedition and all other expeditions to be sent out by other States has been regulated in the best manner by the division into spheres of work.

Vol. XIV, No. 2   WASHINGTON   February, 1903

AMERICAN CLAIMS IN THE ANTARCTIC

DURING the first half of the nineteenth century numerous American seamen explored portions of the South Polar regions and made many and important discoveries there. They named a number of places, and in several instances the lands they discovered were called after them. With the present re-awakened interest in the Antarctic, it is imperatively necessary that American geographers should see to it that American Antarctic discoverers receive due recognition for their discoveries, and that American names should not be crowded off Antarctic charts. It is a pleasure to state that the British Admiralty, in its official charts Nos. 1238 and 1240, shows a desire to be perfectly fair to American explorers, a statement which unfortunately cannot be made of the authors of many semi-official or private English charts. For instance, on the charts in "The Antarctic Manual" of 1901, of all of Wilkes' discoveries only "Knox Land" is marked, and all other American names, including that of Wilkes, are omitted.

In East Antarctica the name "Wilkes Land," and also the names given by Wilkes, "Ringgold Knoll, Eld Peak, Reynolds Peak, Cape Hudson, Point Case, Point Alden, Piner Bay, Cape Carr, North Land, Totten Land, Budd Land, Knox Land," should certainly be marked on all atlases. In West Antarctica there are two American names which require prominent places, "Palmer Land and Pendleton Bay." Nathaniel B. Palmer was probably the discoverer, and certainly the first explorer of the north coast of West Antarctica, and Benjamin Pendleton, before 1828, discovered a great bay or strait on the coast which, not before 1832, received the name of Graham Land.

It would be a great help in obtaining justice for American explorers if an official chart of the Antarctic could be prepared by the United States Hydrographic Office, so as to place officially before the world American claims in the Antarctic, and the National Geographic Society could do no more important work in the next few years than to insist that proper recognition be given to distinguished American Antarctic explorers, and that their names be commemorated by remaining attached to their discoveries.

Edwin Swift Balch.

WORK IN THE FAR SOUTH

THERE are four expeditions at present exploring the far south whose unknown area is greater than twice Europe. The outline map shows the base of operations of three of the parties—the English, the German, and the Scottish; the fourth party, the Swedish, have their base near the Falkland Islands.

Nothing has now been heard from the German expedition for more than a year. They are amply equipped and provisioned and did not expect to send word of their doings before June, 1904.

An auxiliary vessel, the *Morning*, recently entered the Antarctic regions, carrying additional equipment for the British expedition, which is exploring south of New Zealand.

The Scottish expedition, under the command of W. S. Bruce and on board the *Scotia*, sailed from the Falkland Islands for the far south in January, 1903. The other three expeditions have had a year's start of the Scottish expedition, but the latter has an able leader and staff, and will doubtless do equally important work.

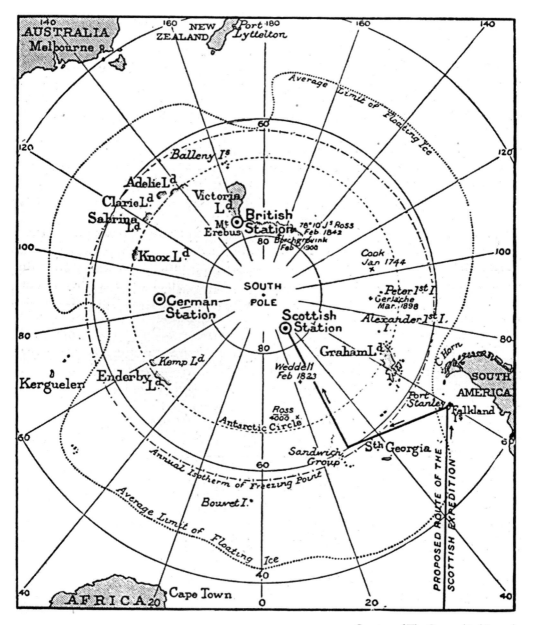

SCOTTISH ANTARCTIC EXPEDITION

THE Chief of the U. S. Weather Bureau has just received a letter from the Scottish Antarctic Expedition, dated January 24th at the Falkland Islands, acknowledging the receipt of assistance from the Weather Bureau. The writer, Mr. R. C. Mossman, meteorologist to the expedition, states: "We leave here tomorrow on the Antarctic ship *Scotia* for the Weddell Sea, pushing south along the 30th parallel of west longitude and wintering in the ice. We do not expect to return here before February or March of next year (1904). I hope to be able to contribute something to the United States Monthly Weather Review. We shall concentrate on kite work as much as circumstances permit, as we have a complete outfit of meteorographs, kites, etc., on board. (This outfit is modeled after that of the U. S. Weather Bureau.) There is, we believe, some possibility of losing a record by the freezing of the ink, as we have not the newly invented ink containing tonsol."

THE BRITISH
SOUTH POLAR EXPEDITION

THE Antarctic expedition sent out by the Royal Geographical Society and Royal Society of England in 1901 has done very good work during its first year in the far south. Captain Scott, the leader, with a sledging party, succeeded in getting 100 miles nearer the South Pole than any predecessor, reaching 80° 17′; the expedition wintered 400 miles further south than any other expedition had ever done before, which makes their meteorological and other scientific observations specially valuable; in their vessel the *Discovery* they coasted along the ice-barrier one hundred and fifty miles beyond the point where James Clarke Ross stopped 60 years ago. This ice-barrier extends from the land out upon the water. From its front, which Captain Scott believes floats on the water, the great southern icebergs break, towering sometimes to nearly 1,000 feet, and compared to which the icebergs of the North Atlantic are but pigmies. After coasting for many days along the ice-front to longitude 152° 30′, latitude 76°, they returned and put in at a safe harbor—Mac-

Murdo Bay. This they made their base of action. Here they passed the winter in sight of Erebus, the volcano which Ross had seen belching forth fire and smoke in 1841. It is quiet now. A sledging party ascended a glacier to the height of 9,000 feet, and found a level plain stretching to the west as far as the eye could reach.

In latitude 82° they discovered an extensive mountainous region, hitherto absolutely unknown, extending to 83° 20′ nearly due south. This discovery seems to indicate that land stretches to the Pole in a series of lofty mountains, and is an important geographical result.

CAPTAIN SCOTT'S REPORT

The *Morning*, the auxiliary wooden ship that left New Zealand December 6, 1902, to carry supplies to Captain Scott, found the expedition at their winter base on Victoria Land, left the provisions, and then returned to New Zealand. The following is Captain Scott's report of his work until the arrival of the *Morning*:

The *Discovery* entered the ice-pack on December 23, 1901, in latitude 67° south. Cape Adare was reached on January 9, but from there a heavy gale and ice delayed the expedition, which did not reach Wood Bay till January 18. A landing was effected on the 20th in an excellent harbor, situated in latitude 76° 30′ south. A record of the voyage was deposited at Cape Crozier on the 22d. The *Discovery* then proceeded along the barrier within a few cables' length, examining the edge and making repeated soundings. In longitude 165° the barrier altered its character and trended northwards. Sounding here showed that the *Discovery* was in shallow water. From the edge of the barrier high snow slopes rose to an extensive, heavily glaciated land, with occasionally bare precipitous peaks. The expedition followed the coast line as far as latitude 76°, longitude 152° 30′. The heavy pack formation of the young ice caused the expedition to seek winter quarters in Victoria Land. On February 3 the *Discovery* entered an inlet in the barrier in longitude 174°. A balloon was sent up and a sledge party examined the land as far as latitude 78° 50′, near Mount Erebus and Terror. At the southern extremity of an island excellent winter quarters were found. The expedition next observed the coast of Victoria Land, extending as far as a conspicuous cape, in latitude 78° 50′. It was found that mountains do not exist here, and the statement that they were to be found is clearly a matter for explanation. Huts for living and for making magnetic observations were erected, and the expedition prepared for wintering. The weather was boisterous, but a reconnaissance of sledge parties was sent out, during which the seaman Vince lost his life, the remainder of the party narrowly escaping a similar fate. The ship was frozen in March 24.

The expedition passed a comfortable winter in well-sheltered quarters. The lowest recorded temperature was 62° below zero. The sledging commenced with the coming of spring, on September 2, parties being sent out in all directions. Lieutenant Royds, Mr. Skelton, and party successfully established a record in an expedition to Mount Terror, traveling over the barrier under severe sledging conditions, with a temperature of 58° below zero. Commander Scott, Dr. Wilson, assistant surgeon, and Lieutenant Shackleton traveled ninety-four miles to the south, reaching land in latitude 80° 18′ south, longitude 163° west, and establishing a world's record for the farthest point south. The journey was accomplished in most trying conditions. The dogs all died, and the three men had to drag the sledges back to the ship. Lieutenant Shackleton almost died from exposure, but is now quite recovered. The party found that ranges of high mountains continued through Victoria Land. At the meridian of 160° foothills much resembling the Admiralty Range were discovered.

The ice barrier is presumably afloat. It continues horizontal and is slowly fed from the land ice. Mountains, ten or twelve thousand feet high, were seen in latitude 82° south, the coast line continuing at least as far as 83° 20′ nearly due south. A party ascending a glacier on the mainland found a new range of mountains. At a height of 9,000 feet a level plain was reached, unbroken to the west as far as the horizon.

The scientific work of the expedition includes a rich collection of marine fauna, of which a large proportion are new species. Sea and magnetic observations were taken, as well as seismographic records and pendulum observations.* A large collection of skins and skeletons of southern seals and sea birds has been made. A number of excellent photographs have been taken and careful meteorological observations were secured. Extensive quartz and grit accumulations were found horizontally bedded in volcanic rocks. Lava flows were found in the frequently recurring plutonic rock which forms the basement of the mountains.

Before the arrival of the *Morning* the *Discovery* had experienced some privation, owing to part of the supplies having gone bad. This accounted for the death of all the dogs. She has, however, revictualled from the *Morning*, and the explorers are now in a position to spend a comfortable winter.

RECORDS OF FARTHEST SOUTH

The following table, compiled by Mr. Cyrus C. Adams, gives the records of the most important Antarctic explorers arranged in the order of the most southerly points attained; it gives the names of the explorers, the year in which they reached their most southerly latitude, the latitude and longitude they attained, the method of reaching it, whether by sledge or ship, and the name of the vessel or vessels in their expeditions:

*It will be interesting to note whether the disturbances of Mont Pelée and La Souffrière, and in Guatemala and Mexico during the past twelve months have been recorded by Captain Scott's instruments or by any of the South Polar expeditions.

S. lat.	Long. from Gr.	
80° 17′	163° 00′ W.	Captain Scott, 1902, sledge, steamer *Discovery*.
78 50	165 00 W.	Borchgrevink, 1900, sledge, steamer *Southern Cross*.
78 10	161 27 W.	Captain James Ross, 1842, ship, sailing vessels *Erebus* and *Terror*.
74 15	34 17 W.	Captain Weddell, 1823, ship, sailing vessels *Jane* and *Beaufoy*.
71 36	87 39 W.	Lieutenant De Gerlache, 1899, ship, steamer *Belgica*.
71 30	15 00 W.	Captain James Ross, 1843, ship, sailing vessels *Erebus* and *Terror*.
71 10	106 54 W.	Captain Cook, 1774, ship, sailing vessels *Resolution* and *Adventure*.
69 53	92 19 W.	Captain Bellingshausen, 1821, ship, sailing vessels *Vostok* and *Mirny*.
69 40	12 00 E.	Captain Biscoe, 1831, ship, sailing vessels *Tula* and *Liveley*.
69 21	2 15 W.	Captain Bellingshausen, 1820, ship, sailing vessels *Vostok* and *Mirny*.
69 10	79 00 W.	Captain Evensen, 1894, ship, sailing vessel *Hertha*.
69 00	172 11 E.	Captain Balleny, 1839, ship, sailing vessels *Eliza Scott* and *Sabrina*.
68 10	60 00 W.	Captain Larsen, 1893, ship, sailing vessel *Jason*.
67 5	147 30 E.	Lieutenant Wilkes, 1840, ship, sailing vessel *Vincennes*.
67 51	39 40 W.	Captain Moore, 1845, ship, sailing vessel *Pagoda*.
67 31	142 54 W.	Captain Cook, 1773, ship, sailing vessels *Resolution* and *Adventure*.

GEOGRAPHIC NOTES

THE SWEDISH SOUTH POLAR EXPEDITION

HON. AUGUSTUS E. INGRAM, Deputy Consul General of the United States at Paris, under date of May 29, sends to the NATIONAL GEOGRAPHIC MAGAZINE the following note of an expedition to be sent out by France in July to rescue the Swedish South Polar Expedition:

When Dr. Otto Nordenskjold set out from Sweden, over a year ago, with a party of thirty-six persons on an expedition for the South Pole, his last words were: "If you are without news of me by April 30, 1903, come to my rescue, for we shall all be in great danger."

That time has come, and no news has been received of Dr. Nordenskjold. In Sweden a relief expedition is being organized, but it cannot start until the end of August. Since this may be too late, and as it is thought that Dr. Nordenskjold's expedition is now in the vicinity of Cape Seymour, which is French soil, the national pride of France has been stirred to be the first to rescue these brave but unfortunate men.

A vessel has already been constructed in France on the lines of the immortal *Fram* and has been named *Le Français*. Dr. Jean Charcot,* well known in French scientific circles, is to command the expedition, and he will be accompanied by other scientists and experienced naval officials. The sum of 150,000 francs is, however, necessary to complete the equipment, and a leading Parisian journal, *Le Matin*, has opened its columns for a subscription list. All classes of people are responding liberally, and it is probable that the French Government, in addition to aid extended by its naval and scientific officials, will also make a contribution of money.

The expedition is expected to leave Havre on the 15th of July, and will without loss of time attempt the work of rescue. When this has been accomplished, *Le Français* will, like the *Fram*, proceed south until it is inclosed in the moving field of ice. At the opportune time a dash across the ice for the South Pole will be made.

*Dr. Charcot had originally intended (as stated in this Magazine, May, 1903) to use his vessel for Arctic rather than South Polar exploration.

This expedition is of especial interest, as it is now nearly three-quarters of a century since France sent an expedition to the South Pole, at which time Dumont d'Urville made considerable discoveries.

* * *

German South Polar Expedition.—The *Gauss*, the steamer of the German South Polar Expedition, has been reported off the east coast of South Africa. Few details of the work of the party have as yet been received, but it would appear that, owing to the ice, they failed to get farther south than 66° 2′, and that the expedition was thus practically a failure. No expense had been spared to make the expedition a success. (It cost $400,000.) The plans had been formed after years of deliberation with the most competent men in Europe. The leader, Captain Drygalski, had proven his ability by previous work in Greenland. Bad luck alone can explain the failure of the expedition and the bitter disappointment of the German nation.

Mr. W. J. Peters, the representative of the National Geographic Society on the Ziegler North Polar Expedition, was presented on his departure with the Society's flag. The flag of the National Geographic Society is of three colors—blue, brown, and green—representing respectively the air, the land, and the water.

* * *

Prof. William H. Brewer, of Yale University, has resigned the presidency of the Arctic Club. He has been president of the Arctic Club since it was founded, eight years ago, and to his leadership is due much of the success of the organization.

The Royal Geographical Society is planning to send south the coming fall an auxiliary vessel to bring back the British South Polar Expedition. According to report, the *Discovery* has been frozen in, and is separated from open water by six miles of ice, which is too great a distance to open with a channel.

THE ANTARCTIC CONTINENT

THAT a vast Antarctic continent exists, perhaps twice as large as Europe, would seem to be proved by the reports now appearing of the recent explorations in that region. The American, Commander Wilkes, returning from the far south in 1841, asserted the existence of a vast South Polar continent, and described his voyage of 1,500 miles in sight of the coast. Ross, however, returning soon after, discredited Wilkes' conclusions, saying that the land seen by Wilkes was merely a great wall of ice. The world has been in doubt which to believe.

That Ross was wrong and Wilkes right is very evident from the report of Captain Scott, of the British Antarctic Expedition of 1901–1904. Captain Scott shows that the mass of ice seen by Ross is in reality an extensive glacier resting on land and covering the land like the ice cap of Greenland. The glacier is about 700 miles wide, and reaches the sea through a plain lying between Victoria Land and Edward VII Land. The German expedition under Von Drygalski, working 80 degrees of longitude farther west, also found a somewhat similar expanse of ice-capped land, whose limits they were unable to trace, but which is apparently a part of the same Antarctic continent.

TERMINATION LAND

The Western End of the Antarctic Continent
Discovered by the American Wilkes

In the deserved congratulations that are being showered on Captain Scott, of the British Antarctic Expedition; Captain Drygalski of the German; Captain Bruce of the Scottish, and Captain Nordenskjold of the Swedish, for their gallant achievements in the Far South, the world is apt to forget that the American naval commander Wilkes discovered in 1840, and first announced to the world the antarctic continent, called "East Antarctica," of which Wilkes Land is a part, and that another American, Captain Palmer, was the pioneer explorer of the opposite side of the antarctic region known as "West Antarctica." The story of the bold ventures of these Americans in puny sailing vessels is told by Mr. Edwin Swift Balch in his "Antarctica," the clearest and most accurate account of south polar exploration that has been published.[1]

O N the 17th of February, 1840, Lieut. Charles Wilkes, U. S. N., at the most westerly point of his memorable cruise which first revealed to the world the existence of a south polar continent, saw appearances of land to the southwest. It was only another point of the continental shore along which he had already sailed for some fifteen hundred miles, and all he says of it is the following sentence:[2] "On the 17th, about 10 a. m., we discovered the barrier extending in a line ahead, and running north and south as far as the eye could reach. Appearances of land were also seen to the southwest, and its trending seemed to be to the northwest. . . . We were now in longitude 97° 37′ E., and latitude 64° 01′ S." Wilkes charted this land as extending from about latitudes 63° 30′ south to 65° south, and from about longitudes 95° west to 97° west, and he gave it the name of Termination Land.

Just recently Dr. Erich von Drygalski published a paper and chart[3] giving the results of

1. Antarctica. E. S. Balch. Philadelphia: Allen, Lane & Scott. 1902.
2. Narrative of the United States Exploring Expedition, Philadelphia, 1845, vol. 2, p. 327.

3. Zeitschrift der Gesellschaft für Erdkundzu Berlin, 1904, No. 1.

the cruise of the *Gauss* to the Antarctic. On his map Dr. von Drygalski charts a coast line, "Hohes Eisbedecktes Land," in about 66° south latitude and 93° west longitude, as discovered by himself. Entirely north of 65° south latitude and entirely east of 95° west longitude he places the words "Termination Land?" In his paper, page 23, Dr. von Drygalski says: "Als Stütze dieser Annahme galt ein von Wilkes als Anschein von Land bezeichnete und mit dem Namen Termination Land belegte sichtung zwischen 95° und 96° Ö. L. v. Gr. und zwischen 64° und 65° S. B., welche jedoch, wie wir heute annehmen müssen, auf Taüschung beruht hat." And at page 26 he writes: "Nach zwei vergeblichen Versuchen, die uns nur über das Nichtvorhandensein von Termination Land kunde brachten." In other words, Dr. von Drygalski coolly proposes to throw out Admiral Wilkes' discoveries entirely in order to take all the credit to himself.

But a comparison of Admiral Wilkes' chart with Dr. von Drygalski's chart shows that the latter's "Hohes Eisbedecktes Land" can be nothing but the west coast of Termination Land; for if on Wilkes' chart we draw a line due southwest from the position of the *Vincennes* on the 17th, this line will go through the center of Termination Land; and if on Drygalski's chart we draw a similar line from the position which he gives of the *Vincennes* on the 17th, this line will go straight to the "Hohes Eisbedecktes Land." The direction tallies exactly. Now, as to distance, the western coast of the "Hohes Eisbedecktes Land," the one which Dr. von Drygalski saw, is about 150 miles from the position of Wilkes on the 17th, and as this land must have some eastward extension and an eastern coast, it is obvious that this eastern side can not be very far from where Wilkes placed Termination Land. Besides, this "eisbedecktes" is also "hohes" land; that is, it is a high, mountainous land, and therefore it must be visible at a long distance. Sir James Clarke Ross states that he sighted Victoria Land at over one hundred miles distance by the land blink, and Wilkes was certainly as near as that to the eastern coast of Termination Land.

Thanks to the voyage of the *Gauss*, therefore, the world now knows positively that Termination Land exists, perhaps a few miles more to the west, but otherwise just about where Admiral Wilkes charted it; and, far from discrediting Admiral Wilkes, the observations of Dr. von Drygalski simply show once more what a remarkably acute and accurate geographical observer Admiral Wilkes was.

EDWIN SWIFT BALCH.

GEOGRAPHIC NOTE

SOME RECENT
ENGLISH STATEMENTS
ABOUT THE ANTARCTIC

IN an article about the English Antarctic Expedition in the *Scottish Geographical Magazine* for May, 1904, at page 265, it is stated that "the *Discovery* succeeded in proving the non-existence of Wilkes Land." In an article by Sir Clements R. Markham, President of the Royal Geographic Society, "The Antarctic Expedition, "in *The Geographical Journal* for May, 1904, at page 551, he states: "On March 2 the *Discovery* passed through the Balleny group. Continuing westward to the 156th meridian, near Adélie Land, it was found that the coast line shown on the chart east of that land is a mistake. No such land exists."

If Captain Scott, after passing through the Balleny Islands, *only sailed as far west as the 156th meridian*, he could at the most have disproved the existence of the extremest western points which Wilkes thought he sighted, namely, Ringgold Knoll and Eld Peak; but as nothing appears to be said so far of the latitude in which the *Discovery* sailed west, even this must remain an open question until further information; and the statement that "the *Discovery* succeeded in proving the non-existence of Wilkes Land," which extends for some fifty-five degrees of longitude west of 156° east longitude, is simply preposterous.

If Captain Scott did not sail west of 156° east longitude, he did not get within some sixteen degrees of longitude, over three hundred miles, of Adélie Land, and he did not approach Cape Hudson, Point Emmons, Point Case, Point Alden, Peacock Bay, and Disappointment Bay, and therefore Sir Clements R. Markham's statement "that the coast line shown on the chart east of that [Adélie] land is a mistake; no such land exists," is entirely unwarranted.

It seems well to call the attention of Americans to this matter, so that they may take cognizance of the fact that some British geographers, led by Sir Clements R. Markham, will perhaps make renewed efforts to smother and obliterate all remembrance of American discoveries in the Antarctic.

Edwin Swift Balch.

Philadelphia, May 21, 1904.

AN ICE WRAPPED CONTINENT*

TO the south of Magellan Strait there is a supposed continent, twice the size of the United States, which is justly called the most mysterious land in the world. During the last few years five expeditions from as many nationalities have sought to unravel the wonders of this vast region, but only one expedition, the British South Polar expedition under command of Captain Robert F. Scott, R. N., has succeeded in getting near enough to do exploring work. This expedition was planned by the Royal Geographical Society of London and assisted financially by the Royal Society and by the British government. It sailed from London July 31, 1901, on *The Discovery*, which had been especially built for the work, and returned to England September 10, 1904. An unfortunate attack of scurvy during the first year, caused by tinned meats, and the fact that three relief ships were sent after it, unnecessarily it developed af-

*A review of "The Voyage of *The Discovery*," by Captain Robert F. Scott, with 260 full-page and smaller illustrations, by Dr. E. A. Wilson and others, 14 colored plates, and 2 maps. 2 vols., 556 and 508 pages. New York: Imported by Charles Scribner's Sons.

terward, at first somewhat dampened the enthusiasm with which the discoveries of the expedition were received, but the scientific reports now appearing show that immense additions have been made to our knowledge of the "bottom of the globe."

Captain Scott was very wise as well as fortunate in his choice of base, which he established at the western end of the great ice barrier, under the shadow of two lofty snow-clad volcanoes, Mounts Terror and Erebus, which Ross had seen in state of violent eruption 60 years before. To the east stretched the unending plain of the ice barrier, while to the west towered a great range of mountains, with peaks 9,000 feet in height. The first year efforts were concentrated in exploring the ice barrier, and the second to discovering what lay behind the chain of mountains.

THE GREAT ICE BARRIER

"Perhaps of all the problems which lay before us in the south, we were most keenly interested in solving the mysteries of this great ice-mass. Sixty years before, Ross's triumphant voyage to the south had been abruptly termi-

THE GREAT ICE BARRIER

Captain Scott sailed for 500 miles along this continuous cliff of ice, which rises from 10 to 280 feet above the sea. He also traveled 400 miles over it straight into the interior—from 78° to 82° 17′ south latitude—but even then did not reach or see its end. The barrier is afloat, but is apparently wearing away at the rate of about one-half mile a year. Captain Scott reports that it has receded 30 miles since Sir James Ross examined its front.

nated by a frowning cliff of ice, which he traced nearly 400 miles to the east; such a phenomenon was unique, and for sixty years it had been discussed and rediscussed, and many a theory had been built on the slender foundation of fact which alone the meager information concerning it could afford."

Before taking *The Discovery* to her permanent quarters, Captain Scott coasted along the entire front of this barrier, and determined that it extended from the volcanoes Erebus and Terror for nearly 500 miles to an ice-clad land on the west, which he discovered and named King Edward VII Land. When he afterward charted the track of the ship he found he had sailed from 20 to 30 miles farther south than Ross had done; in other words, that 20 to 30 miles of ice barrier had worn off since Ross had seen it.

At one point he halted the ship and moored her to the barrier for a day, while different members of the staff ascended in a captive balloon to 800 feet elevation. While lying alongside the ice wharf for 24 hours, the ship and wharf rose and fell together. The depth of water here was 315 fathoms.

EXAMINING THE ICE BARRIER FROM A BALLOON

Captain Scott makes the important observation that the surface current set into the barrier and under the ice for a certain time, then turned and set out again to sea. It would be very interesting to know how far "inland" this flux and reflux penetrates.

During the first spring and summer Captain Scott, Lieutenant Schackleton, and Dr. Wilson advanced 400 miles due south across the barrier to 82° 17′ south latitude. When they halted they could see to at least 84°, but the barrier still stretched ahead, apparently unending. If the dogs had not failed the party, they would probably have succeeded in getting farther, but, as it is, they beat the record for the "Farthest South" by several degrees.

This ice barrier is probably thrust off of some great body of land enveloping the South Pole. While the barrier is wearing away in front, as proven by the fact of its retreat of 30 miles in 60 years, it is being constantly fed in the rear; in fact, its recession in front would be considerably more rapid if the loss was not balanced by additions in the rear.* How far off the source is, is a mystery; and when we bear in mind the scarcity of precipitation in such southern latitudes, it is almost impossible to imagine where the supply is to be found.

The following year Lieutenant Royds led a party about 100 miles across the barrier to the east. Like Scott, he found it level everywhere.

It was on this journey also that a most interesting series of magnetic observations were taken by Bernacchi, who carried with him the Barrow dip circle, an especially delicate instrument. The great value of these observations lies in the fact that they were taken in positions which were free from all possible disturbances, either from casual iron or from land masses; the positions also run in a line which is almost directly away from the Magnetic Pole, and consequently the series is an invaluable aid to map-

*Voyage of *The Discovery*, vol. 2, p. 421.

ping out the magnetic conditions of the whole of this region.

THE MOST DESOLATE LAND IN THE WORLD

During the entire march of 400 miles southward over the ice barrier, Captain Scott had been flanked by a lofty mountain chain on the right at a distance of about 50 to 30 miles. The peaks he named after prominent Englishmen and supporters of the expedition, Mount Markham (15,000), Mount Longstaff (10,350), etc. At the end of the march he had tried to reach this land, but an immense chasm (below) barred his way. On his return to the ship, after an absence of 93 days, he found that Lieutenant Armitage had discovered a route across this chain of mountains, beyond which he reported a limitless ice-covered plateau at an elevation of 8,900 feet and flat as a table. Armitage, however, did not attempt to advance across the plain. The following year Captain Scott and several companions ascended to this plateau by Armitage's route. Their dogs had all failed and the men were obliged to drag the heavy sledges. It was a heavy pull, as they had to climb 9,000 feet in 70 miles, up a rough glacier.

Captain Scott traveled to the westward about 200 miles across this plateau, which did not vary in altitude more than 60 or 70 feet. At

THE CHASM WHICH PREVENTED CAPTAIN SCOTT FROM REACHING LAND
AT THE END OF HIS 400-MILE MARCH UP THE ICE BARRIER

one point he passed directly south of the Magnetic Pole.

"The error of our compass had passed from east to west and was nearly at its maximum of 180°; although I could not calculate it accurately at the time, I could get a good idea of its amount by observing the direction in which the sun reached its greatest altitude. The reader will see that from a magnetic point of view this was a very interesting region. We were directly south of the South Magnetic Pole and the north end of our compass needle was pointing toward the South (geographical) Pole.

"To show what a practical bearing this reversal of the compass had, I may remark that in directing Skelton on his homeward track to the eastward, I told him to steer due west by the compass card. It is only on this line or the similar one which joins the northern poles that such an order could be given, and we were not a little proud of being the first to experience this distinctly interesting physical condition in the Southern Hemisphere.

"There can be little doubt, I think, that the wind blows from the west to the east across this plateau throughout the winter, and often with great violence, as the high snow-waves show.

ADVANCING OVER THE GREAT INLAND PLATEAU

Nine thousand feet above the sea, discovered by Scott and Armitage. The most desolate land in the world, where the temperature in midsummer often falls to 40 degrees below zero.

What the temperature can be at that season is beyond guessing; but if the thermometer can fall to −40° in the height of the summer, one can imagine that the darker months produce a terrible extremity of cold.

"The interior of Victoria Land must be considered the most desolate region in the world. There is none other that is at once so barren, so deserted, so piercingly cold, so windswept, or so fearsomely monotonous.

"When the reader considers its geographical situation, its great elevation, and the conditions to which we were subjected while traveling across it, he will, I think, agree that there can be no place on earth that is less attractive.

"This great ice-sheet is unique; it has no parallel in the world, and its discovery must be looked upon as a notable geographic fact."

ICE-FLOWERS

In his diary, Captain Scott gives the following description of the only flowers they saw:

"*March 30 (Easter Sunday)*.—Like yesterday, a fine day, with a light northerly breeze. This is a season of flowers, and behold! they have sprung up about us as by magic—very beautiful ice-flowers, waxen white in the shadow, but radiant with prismatic colors, where the sun rays light on their delicate petals. It was a phenomenon to be expected in the newly frozen sea, but it is curious that they should come to their greatest perfection on this particular day. The ice is about five inches thick and free from snow; consequently the ice-flowers stand up clear-cut and perfect in form. In some places they occur thickly, with broad, delicate, feathery leaves; in others the dark, clear ice surface is visible, with only an occasional plant on it; in others, again, the plants assume a spiky appearance, being formed of innumerable small spicules.

"The more nearly one examines these beautiful formations, the more wonderful they appear, as it is only by close inspection that the mathematical precision of the delicate tracery can be observed. It is now established that on the freezing of salt water much of the brine is mechanically excluded. Sea-ice is much less salt than the sea itself, and what salt remains is supposed only to be entangled in the frozen water. The amount of salt excluded seems to depend on the rate at which the ice is formed, and while some is excluded below the ice-surface, some is also pushed out above, and it is this that forms the ice-flowers. The subject is very fascinating, and we have already started to measure the salinity of ice taken from different depths and formed under various conditions; the ice-flowers themselves do not seem to constitute a saturated solution of brine, and why they should differ in form in various places seems beyond explanation."

THE EMPEROR PENGUIN

"We had felt that this penguin was the truest type of our region. All other birds fled north when the severity of winter descended upon us; the Emperor was alone prepared to face the extremest rigors of our climate; and we gathered no small satisfaction from being the first to throw light on the habits of a creature that so far surpasses in hardiness all others of the feathered tribe.*

"Not many birds undertake to lay their eggs in the darkness of a polar winter, nor do many birds appear to think that sea-ice is the

3. This description of this remarkable bird is from the chapter on "Antarctic Fauna," by Edmund A. Wilson. Voyage of *The Discovery*, vol. 2, p. 469.

A PRESSURE RIDGE ALONG THE COAST

most attractive ground to 'sit' on. And when, in addition to this, we find the Emperor penguin hatching out its chicks in the coldest month of the whole Antarctic year, when the mean temperature for the month is 18° below zero, Fahrenheit, and the minimum may fall to −68°, I think we may rightly consider the bird to be eccentric.

"The Emperor penguin stands nearly four feet high, and weighs upward of 80 to 90 pounds. He is an exceedingly handsome bird, with a rich black head, a bluish-gray back and wings, a lemon-yellow breast, with a satin-like gloss on the feathers, and a brilliant patch of orange on the neck and lower bill. His movements are slow and stately, and the dignity of his appearance is much increased by the up-

right carriage of his head and bill. When a group of these birds is met with in the middle of the desert ice, where all around is gray and cold and white and silent, the richness of their coloring strikes one very forcibly. Their voice is loud and trumpet-like, and rings out in the pack-ice with a note of defiance that makes one feel that man is the real intruder. They have no fear, but an abundance of inquisitiveness, and a party such as I have mentioned will walk up to one with dignity, and stand in a ring all round, with an occasional remark from one to the other, discussing, no doubt, the nature of this new and upright neighbor.

"The method employed by the Emperor penguin for carrying the egg and chick upon his feet is shared also by the King penguin of the

THE HUNTER WAITING
FOR A SEAL TO COME UP TO BREATHE

sub-Antarctic area; as we saw in our visit to their rookeries in the Macquarie Islands. The King penguin we saw as he sat in mud and puddles, with his single egg upon his feet, and now we saw the Emperor penguin doing precisely the same thing with his single chicken to keep it off the ice; and we are agreed that the term 'pouch,' which has been used in this connection, is one which not only does not describe the matter, but is anatomically wrong and misleading. The single egg, or the chick, sits resting on the dorsum of the foot, wedged in between the legs and the lower abdomen, and over it falls a fold of heavily feathered skin, which is very loose, and can completely cover up and hide the egg or chick from view. When the chick is hungry or inquisitive, it pokes out from under the maternal (or paternal) lappet a piebald downy head of black and white, emitting its shrill and persistent pipe until the mother (or the father) fills it up.

"The feeding is managed as with cormorants and many other birds, the little one finding regurgitated food when it thrusts its head inside the parent's mouth.

"I think the chickens hate their parents, and when one watches the proceedings in a rookery it strikes one as not surprising. In the first place, there is about one chick to ten or twelve adults, and each adult has an overpowering desire to 'sit' on something. Both males and females want to nurse, and the result is that when a chicken finds himself alone there is a rush on the part of a dozen unemployed to seize him. Naturally, he runs away, and dodges here and there till a six-stone Emperor falls on him, and then begins a regular football 'scrimmage,' in which each tries to hustle the other off, and the end is too often disastrous to the chick. Sometimes he falls into a crack in the ice, and stays there to be frozen while the parents squabble at the top; sometimes, rather than be nursed, I have seen him crawl in under an ice-ledge and remain there, where the old ones could not reach him. I think it is not an exaggeration to say that of the 77 per cent that die, no less than half are killed by kindness."

SOME INTERESTING OBSERVATIONS

The power of the midnight sun in these latitudes is illustrated by the fact that when several members of a party were caught on a ice-

A WANDERING ALBATROSS
CAUGHT ON THE VOYAGE SOUTH

never satisfactorily explained this matter. The seal seems to crawl to the shore or the ice to die, possibly from its instinctive dread of its marine enemies; but unless we had actually found these remains, it would have been past believing that a dying seal could have transported itself over fifty miles of rough steep glacier surface."

The dogs which had been brought from Siberia had the unpleasant experience of molting in winter, which was the Arctic summer, but their fur soon came out again.

The members of the party kept up their good spirits by outdoor games. One of the most spirited contests was a game of hockey April 7 by "The Married and Engaged *vs.* The Single," the match being played in a temperature of −40°.

AMERICAN EXPLORERS OVERLOOKED

Every one who reads Captain Scott's narrative as given in "The Voyage of *The Discovery*" must admire the strong and hearty personality of the leader. He is full of energy, and not only did the hardest work himself, but was able to get others to follow him willingly and cheerfully. His lieutenants and men likewise command our respect for their courage, fidelity, and faithful work.

It is unfortunate, however, that in his résumé of what has been done in the far south by previous explorers he completely overlooks the two Americans who discovered the Antarctic

floe for several hours without matches, Dr. Wilson was able to produce a light for their pipes from a small pocket magnifying glass. During the summer the biologist of the staff succeeded in growing a crop of mustard and cress. He raised some on flannel and with chemicals, but the best result was obtained from Antarctic soil, "which is evidently most productive."

No vegetation of any kind was seen anywhere, but, on the other hand, they found an abundance of animal life, so that no party wintering in the Antarctic regions will have difficulty in providing themselves with fresh food.

On their ascent to the inland plateau they "passed two more carcasses of Weddell seals; the last was at the greatest altitude we have yet found one, nearly 5,000 feet above the sea; it grows more than ever wonderful how these creatures can have got so far from the sea. We

THE AURORA AUSTRALIS

Continent—Palmer, who first saw the western half of the continent, now called West Antarctica, and Admiral Charles Wilkes, who first sighted and defined the eastern half of the continent, known as Wilkes' Land.

To quote Major General A. W. Greely, U. S. Army:

"Captain Scott is happier as an explorer than as an historian. From his narrative and charts is absent the name of the American who

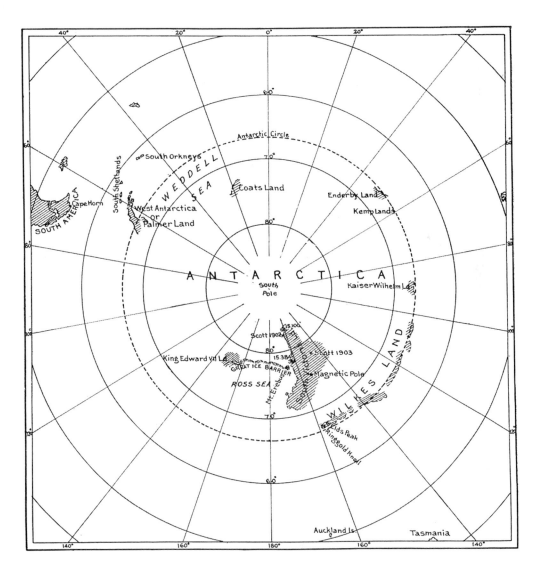

OUTLINE MAP OF SOUTH POLAR REGIONS

discovered the Antarctic Continent, Captain N. B. Palmer. Further, not only does Scott omit mention of Palmer and erase his name from the Antarctic map, but he gives the credit for the first discovery of land in the Antarctic regions to the distinguished Russian navigator, Bellinghausen.

"The discovery in the summer of 1820–1821 of Palmer Land, from the summit of Deception Island, South Shetlands, is described in Fanning's Voyages, p. 435. Captain N. B. Palmer, in the sloop *Hero*, visited this land, and on his return passage fell in with Bellinghausen, whom Palmer informed of the mountainous land to the south."

But more remarkable was the voyage of Admiral Charles Wilkes, in 1840. To quote Edwin S. Balch, author of "Antarctica:"*

"With unsuitable, improperly equipped ships, amid icebergs, gales, snowstorms, and fogs, Wilkes followed an unknown coast line for over 1,500 miles, a distance exceeding in length the Ural Mountains. It is the long distance which Wilkes traversed which makes the results of his cruise so important, for he did not merely sight the coast in one or two places, but he hugged it for such a distance as to make sure that the land was continental in dimensions. The expedition noticed appearances of land on

*NATIONAL GEOGRAPHIC MAGAZINE, 1903.

January 13; it sighted land almost surely on January 16, from 157° 46′ east longitude, and again more positively on January 19, from 154° 30′ east longitude, 66° 20′ south latitude. On January 30 the size of the land was sufficiently ascertained to receive the name 'Antarctic Continent,' and this discovery of Wilkes is the most important discovery yet made in the Antarctic."

Impartial geographers in due time recognized the importance of Wilkes' discovery, and in recognition of his work affixed the name Wilkes Land to the portion of the Antarctic Continent along which he coasted.

The homeward track of *The Discovery* disproved the existence of merely a small part of Wilkes Land, namely, Eld Peak and Ringold's Knoll, to the east of Adelie, but Captain Scott adds that "whilst it is certain that we must reject Wilkes Land to the eastward of Adelie Land, Wilkes' soundings still remain as a guide to the limit of the continental plateau in this region. Our own uniform soundings of 250 fathoms, together with his, show that there is considerable extent of shallow sea, limited more or less by the track of the Wilkes' ships, approximately along the Antarctic Circle."

The German South Polar expedition confirmed the opposite end of Wilkes Land in 1902.

G. H. G.

GEOGRAPHIC NOTE

MOTOR SLEDGES
IN THE ANTARCTIC

A NEW South Polar Expedition is being organized by Lieutenant E. H. Shackleton, who was a member of the recent British expedition and also one of the sledging party who reached farthest south, 82° 17′. Mr. Shackleton plans to leave England October of this year on a steam whaler, and to establish his winter quarters at the station used by the *Discovery* near Mount Erebus. His party will be limited to from nine to twelve men. Mr. Shackleton introduces two innovations: The use of Siberian ponies, which Fiala found so useful in the north, and a specially designed motor car for traveling over the ice barrier. Mr. Shackleton in his announcement says:

"A North China or Siberian pony is capable of dragging 1,800 pounds on a food basis of 10 pounds per day. A dog drags 100 pounds at the outside, and requires over 2 pounds of food per day. Therefore one pony drags as much as eighteen dogs, at less than one-third in weight of provision, and can travel comfortably 20 to 25 miles per day.

"The motor will be of a special type, taking into consideration the temperatures to be encountered and the surface to be traveled over. I would propose to take three or four ponies on the southern journey and the motor car. As long as the car continued to remain satisfactory, it alone would be used to drag our equipment and provisions. If it broke down and could not be fixed up, then the ponies would take over the load.

"I would propose traveling at the rate of 20 to 25 miles a day, and feel assured that, providing the motor does its work, 82° 16′ S. I intend, every 100 miles, to drop a sledge load of provisions and equipment; so that, in the event of every means of traction breaking down except the men, we would only have 100 miles to go between each depot on return. The geographical South Pole is 731 miles from winter quarters, and allowing that we only go with the motor to 82° 16′ S., we would then practically be starting for the remaining 464 miles as fresh as if we were starting from the ship. What lies beyond 83° S. we cannot tell, but I am of the opinion that we can follow the trend of the southern mountains for a very long way south before they turn either east or west."

GEOGRAPHIC NOTE

AN AMERICAN
SOUTH POLAR EXPEDITION

THE following communication from Commander Robert Edwin Peary, U. S. N., was presented by Herbert L. Bridgman, acting delegate of the United States of America to the Polar Congress recently held in Brussels:

"I beg to state that on my return from my coming Arctic expedition I shall endeavor, in every possible way consistent with my other duties, to promote and organize a national American Antarctic expedition to secure for this country its share of the honors and valuable scientific information still awaiting the explorer in that region.

"The project would include the building of another special ship on the same general lines and in the light of the experience gained in building and using the *Roosevelt*, and the utilization of the methods and equipment evolved during my past seventeen years of Arctic work. It would not contemplate my personal association with the expedition in the field.

"While it is too early now to make any definite statement, it is hoped that the Peary Arctic Club may lend its encouragement to the work.

"This project, I am happy to state, has the approval of President Roosevelt.

"At a subsequent session of the commission it is hoped to offer a more detailed presentation of the matter for such action or suggestions as the commission may see fit."

SHACKLETON'S FARTHEST SOUTH

ALL records for South Polar exploration have been surpassed by Lieut. E. H. Shackleton, R. N., who is now returning to England after fourteen months spent within the Antarctic Circle. Shackleton, on January 9, 1909, gained a point within 111 miles from the South Geographical Pole, while another of his parties actually reached the South Magnetic Pole on January 16, 1909, according to press dispatches from New Zealand. He has shown that the Geographical Pole is situated on a high plateau about 10,000 feet above sealevel, and that the remarkable floating ice-barrier stretching for 500 miles between King William VII Land and Victoria Land, and justly called one of the wonders of the world, does not apparently reach beyond the eighty-third degree. But to Americans his most interesting discovery is new land and mountain ranges extending from South Victoria Land, which once more confirms the great discoveries of the American Wilkes, made nearly seventy years ago. (See pages 49–50).

Lieutenant Shackleton, with a party of about 15 men, dogs, Siberian ponies, motor cars, and other equipment, was landed from the *Nimrod* in January, 1908, at Cape Royds, near the base of the smoking volcano, Mount Erebus. Here he made his headquarters for the year at the same base used by the previous British Antarctic Expedition (1901–1904), led by Captain Scott, whose splendid achievements were described in this Magazine in February, 1907. The motor cars proved apparently of little value during the ensuing year's work, owing to the crevasses in the ice, but the Siberian ponies showed remarkable endurance of cold and great pulling power.

Campaigning against the Pole in some respects is easier in the south than in the north. The weather is much harsher and more boisterous in the south, but the working season is longer. The North Pole is surrounded by an ice-covered ocean, which must be crossed in spring before the ice breaks apart under the summer sun. The South Pole, on the other hand, is situated on a great ice plateau, which may be traversed during almost the entire period of daylight. Thus, while Peary must complete his dash from the most northern land to the Pole and back in a period of about sixty days, the South Polar explorer has more than one hundred and twenty days at his disposal.

Lieutenant Shackleton not only won the record for farthest south, but he has reached a point nearer the South Pole than any explorer has been able to approach to the North Pole. The story of his year's work, as given in the cable dispatches from New Zealand, follows:

The southern party—Adams, Marshall, Wild, and I—with four ponies and a supporting party, consisting of Sir Philip Brocklehurst and Messrs. Joyce, Marson, Armytage, and Priestly, left Cape Royds on October 29, 1908, with ninety-one days' provisions. The supporting party returned on November 7.

Owing to the bad light among the ice crevasses, Adams and a pony were nearly lost. We reached on November 13 the depot laid out in September in latitude 79° 36′, longitude 168° east. We took on a pony the maize and provisions previously left there and commenced reducing our daily rations.

We traveled south along meridian 168 over a varying surface, high ridges and mounds of snow alternating with soft snow. The ponies often sank to their bellies. In latitude 81° 4′ we shot the pony Chinaman and made a depot of oil, biscuit, and pony meat. The remainder of the pony meat we took on to eke out our dried rations.

On November 26 we reached the *Discovery* expedition's southernmost latitude. The surface was now extremely soft, with large undulations. The ponies were attacked with snow blindness. On November 28 the pony Grisi was shot. We made a depot in latitude 82° 45′, longitude 170°. The pony Quan was shot on November 30. We had now traveled 400 miles across the ice barrier.

Steering south and southeast, we were now approaching a high range of new mountains trending to the southeast. We found on December 2 the barrier influenced by great pressure and the ridges of snow and ice turned into land. We discovered a glacier 120 miles long and approximately 40 miles wide, running in a south and southwesterly direction.

ASCENT TO THE CONTINENTAL PLATEAU

We started on December 5 to ascend the glacier at latitude 83° 33′, longitude 172°. The glacier was badly crevassed as the result of huge pressure. The surface on December 6 was so crevassed that it took the whole day to fight our way 600 yards.

On December 7 the pony Socks, breaking through a snow lid, disappeared in a crevasse of unknown depth. The swingletree snapping, we saved Wild and the sledge, which was damaged. The party was now hauling a weight of 250 pounds per man.

The clouds disappearing on December 8, we discovered new mountain ranges trending south and southwest. Moving up the glacier over the treacherous snow covering the crevasses, we frequently fell through, but were saved by our harness and were pulled out with the Alpine rope. A second sledge was badly damaged by knife-edged crevasses.

Similar conditions obtained on our way up the glacier from December 18, when we reached an altitude of 6,800 feet. In latitude 85° 10′ we made a depot and left everything there but our food, instruments, and camp equipment, and reduced rations to twenty ounces per man daily.

We reached on December 26 a plateau, after crossing ice falls, at an altitude of 9,000 feet, thence rising gradually in long ridges to 10,500 feet.

Finishing the relay work, we discarded our second sledge. There was a constant southerly

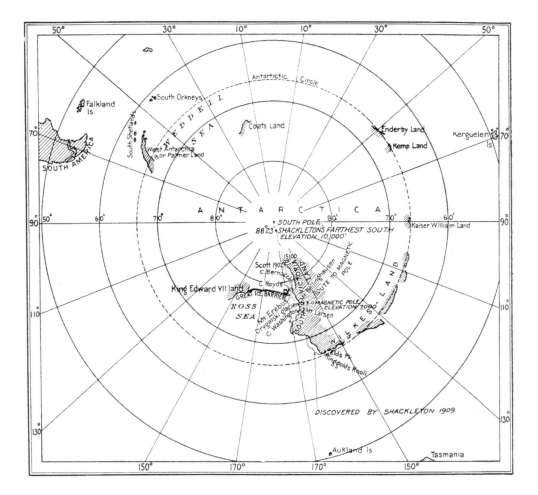

OUTLINE MAP OF SOUTH POLAR REGIONS

blizzard, wind, and drifting snow, with the temperature ranging from 37 to 70 degrees of frost. We lost sight of the new mountains on December 27.

Finding the party weakening from the effects of the shortage of food and rarefied air and cold, I decided to risk making a depot on the plateau. We proceeded on January 4 with one tent, utilizing the poles of the second tent for guiding marks for our return. The surface became soft and the blizzard continued.

WITHIN 111 MILES OF THE POLE

For sixty hours during January 7, 8, and 9 the blizzard raged, with 72° of frost and the wind blowing seventy miles an hour. It was impossible to move. Members of the party were frequently frostbitten in their sleeping bags. We left camp on January 9 and reached latitude 88° 23′, longitude 162°.

This is the most southerly point ever reached. Here we hoisted the Union Jack presented to us by the Queen. No mountains were visible. We saw a plain stretching to the south.

We returned to pick up our depot on the plateau, guided by our outward tracks, for the flags attached to the tent poles had been blown away. Less violent blizzards blowing at our backs helped us to travel from twenty to twenty-nine miles daily. We reached the upper glacier depot on January 19.

The snow had been blown from the glacier surface, leaving slippery, blue ice. The descent was slow work in the heavy gale. The sledge was lowered by stages by the Alpine rope.

On the morning of January 26 our food was finished. It was slow going. Sixteen miles were covered in twenty-two hours' march. The snow was two feet deep, concealing the crevasses. We reached the lower glacier depot in latitude 83° 45′ on the afternoon of January 27. There we obtained food and, proceeding, reached the Grisi depot, named after the dead pony, on February 2.

There was no food remaining. Wild was suffering from dysentery, the effect of horse meat. The entire party were prostrated by dysentery on February 4 and were unable to move. The dysentery continued eight days, but helped by strong southerly blizzards we reached Chinaman depot on February 13. The food had again run out.

The blizzards continued, with 50° of frost. We discarded everything except our camp outfit and geological specimens and on February 20 reached the next depot, all our food being finished.

Helped by the southerly blizzard, which was accompanied by 67° of frost, we reached on February 23 a depot on Minna Bluff, which had been laid by the Joyce party in January. Here we received news from the ship. Marshall had a relapse and return of dysentery.

We made a forced march of twenty-four miles on February 26. Marshall was suffering greatly. On February 27 Marshall was unable to march. I left him in camp in charge of Adams, while Wild and I made a forced march to the ship for relief. I returned on March 1 with a relief party, and all reached the ship at Hut Point on March 4 in a blizzard.

The total distance of the journey, including relays, was 1,708 statute miles. The time occupied was 126 days. The main result is a good geological collection. We found coal measures in limestone. We also made a complete meteorological record. We discovered eight distinct mountain ranges and more than a hundred mountains. We surveyed and photographed many glaciers and found signs of former greater glaciation.

The Geographical South Pole is doubtless situated on a plateau, from 10,000 to 11,000 feet above the sea level. The new mountains' altitudes range from 3,000 to 12,000 feet approximately. The violent blizzards in latitude 88° show that if the "polar calm" exists it must be in a small area or is not coincident with the Geographic Pole.

LOCATING THE MAGNETIC POLE

The northern party, consisting of Douglas, Marson, Rackay, and Davis, left Cape Royds for the Magnetic Pole on October 5, 1908. We picked up the depot left by the motor car fifteen miles out. The party hauled two sledges by relays, the total weight being 600 pounds per man, with provisions for ninety-three days.

The thawing sea ice, compacted of brush and crushed pack, made progress laborious and slow. The sea ice south of the Drygalski Glacier was beginning to break up. The first attempt to cross to the glacier failed, owing to numerous deep chasms. We crossed further east on December 6, and followed a difficult route over crevassed pressure ridges.

We attempted the glacier between the mountains Nansen and Larsen. After sledging among high pressure ridges, where the sledges and party were often nearly lost in the crevasses, we abandoned that route. A blizzard then covered the glacier deeply drifted with snow and the sledges were extricated with difficulty.

Subsequently violent blizzards removing the loose snow enabled the party to ascend the steep slope of a branch glacier to the main glacier between the mountains Larsen and Bellinghausen. Thence there was fair traveling to an inland plateau at an altitude of over 7,000 feet. Strong southerly winds, 50° of frost, and shortened rations made traveling trying.

The party reached the Magnetic Pole, 260 statute miles northwest of the Drygalski depot, on January 16, and hoisted the Union Jack. The position of the Pole was determined by Marson with a Lloydreak dip circle as in the vicinity of latitude 72° 25′, longitude 15° 4′ east.

The duration of the journey was 122 days. We traveled, including relays, 1,260 statute miles. The coast was triangulated by Marson with a theodolite from McMurdo to the Drygalski Glacier. There are also geological, magnetic, and meteorological results. Minerals, apparently vanadium and widely spread monastite, were found.

In March, 1908, a party headed by Lieut. Adams, left Cape Royds to ascend Erebus, the great Antarctic volcano. They climbed with a sledge to an altitude of 5,500 feet, thence carrying their equipment on their backs. They reached an altitude of 9,500 feet on March 7. The temperature was 50° below freezing. Then a violent blizzard raged for thirty hours. Resuming the ascent on March 9, they reached the old crater of the volcano at over 11,000 feet.

Unique fumaroles or smokeholes were found. The old crater was chiefly filled with large felspar crystals, pumice and sulphur. Sir Philip Brocklehurst had both feet badly frostbitten. One toe was subsequently amputated. The summit was reached on March 10. The active crater is half a mile in diameter and 800 feet deep. It was ejecting vast volumes of steam and sulphurous gas to a height of 2,000 feet.

WILKE'S DISCOVERIES CONFIRMED

The *Nimrod* on the voyage to pick up the expedition reached the ice sheet off Mt. Erebus on January 3. Various parties of the expedition 2were taken on board at different points, Lieut. Shackleton's being the last, on March 4.

On the voyage homeward in the *Nimrod* from latitude 69° 48′, longitude 166° 11′, they discovered a new range of coast mountains trending first southwest and then west. The approximate altitude of these mountains is from 5,000 to 7,000 feet. They are mostly tabular and form part of an apparently deeply eroded plateau. This discovery by Shackleton is an extension of South Victoria Land westward to about 70° 30′ south, 162° east, which appears to render certain its continuity with Wilkes Land.

Gen. A. W. Greely, in his admirable "Handbook of Polar Discoveries," successfully demonstrates the general correctness of Wilkes' discoveries, which were acrimoniously disputed by Captain Ross, R. N., whose own Parry Mountains have been proved non-existent. The very high land seen by Wilkes, when he discovered the Antarctic continent, on January 19, 1840, is only separated from Shackleton's discovery by about 250 miles.

The ends of the globe are as far apart in character as in distance. General Greely, in his "Handbook of Polar Discoveries," gives the following interesting comparison of the polar areas:

The lands within the Arctic Circle are not alone contiguous to powerful and enterprising nations, but are also so favored by climate and soil as to present suitable conditions for animal and plant life. Indeed, Arctic Europe, Asia, and America present large habitable districts, where human activities afford life environments not altogether harsh or unattractive. In addition the northern seas, filled with abundant life, furnish subsistence and wealth to thousands of daring men who yearly seek their accessible waters.

At the other Pole of the world we find the Antarctic region to be the true land of desolation—forbidding, inaccessible, and uninhabitable. Its northern confines and surroundings are largely oceanic, so that freezing temperatures, fierce snow-blizzards, and other winter conditions are not unusual in midsummer. While in high latitude near the South Pole there are extended lands and doubtless a continent, yet these are sterile areas, overlaid with ice-coverings of vast extent and enormous thickness.

It is doubtful if one per centum of Antarctic lands is ever ice-free, so that ordinary forms of land-life are absolutely wanting. Not only are human inhabitants unknown south of Cape Horn, more than 2,300 miles from the Pole, but, except sea forms, within the circle animal life and vegetable life are practically absent save a few low forms of hardy lichens and mosses. No plant life gladdens the eye, and even the hum of insects is unheard, the terrestrial fauna consisting of wingless insects. Sea life is more abundant than in any other ocean, the higher forms being whales, seals, and birds—skuas, penguins, and petrels—but owing to distance and danger their pursuit and capture are no longer remunerative.

THE HEART OF THE ANTARCTIC

By Lieut. Ernest H. Shackleton

In the April, 1909, number of the National Geographic Magazine there was printed a summary of the geographical results of Lieutenant Shackleton's South Polar Expedition of 1908–09. The narrative of the extraordinary achievements of his party, which included reaching a point within 110 miles of the South Pole, attaining the South Magnetic Pole, and climbing the lofty summit of the volcano, Mount Erebus, is published this month by J. B. Lippincott Company of Philadelphia, and by courtesy of the publishers the following extracts and illustrations are reprinted here.

Lieutenant Shackleton tells the story of his work simply and modestly in two handsome volumes, beautifully illustrated from photographs and with large maps in colors. An introduction by Hugh Robert Mill summarizes the work of previous south polar expeditions.

MEN go out into the void spaces of the world for various reasons. Some are actuated simply by a love of adventure, some have the keen thirst for scientific knowledge, and others again are drawn away from the trodden paths by the "lure of little voices," the mysterious fascination of the unknown. I think that in my own case it was a combination of these factors that determined me to try my fortune once again in the frozen south.

I had been invalided home before the conclusion of the *Discovery* expedition, and I had a very keen desire to see more of the vast continent that lies amid the Antarctic snows and glaciers. Indeed, the stark polar lands grip the hearts of the men who have lived on them in a manner that can hardly be understood by the people who have never got outside the pale of civilization.

The *Discovery* expedition had gained knowledge of the great chain of mountains running in a north and south direction from Cape Adare to latitude 82° 17′ south, but whether this range turned to the southeast or eastward for any con-

THE "NIMROD" PUSHING THROUGH HEAVY PACK ICE
ON HER WAY SOUTH, CARRYING THE SHACKLETON PARTY

siderable distance was not known, and therefore the southern limits of the Great Ice Barrier plain had not been defined.

The glimpses gained of King Edward VII Land from the deck of the *Discovery* had not enabled us to determine either its nature or its extent, and the mystery of the Barrier remained unsolved. It was a matter of importance to the scientific world that information should be gained regarding the movement of the ice-sheet that forms the Barrier. Then I wanted to find out what lay beyond the mountains to the south of latitude 82° 17′ and whether the Antarctic continent rose to a plateau similar to the one found by Captain Scott beyond the Western Mountains.

There was much to be done in the field of meteorology, and this work was of particular importance to Australia and New Zealand, for these countries are affected by weather conditions that have their origin in the Antarctic. Antarctic zoology, though somewhat limited, as regarded the range of species, had very interesting aspects, and I wanted to devote some attention to mineralogy, apart from general geology.

The Aurora Australis, atmospheric electricity, tide movements, hydrography, currents of the air, ice formations and movements, biology and geology, offered an unlimited field for research, and the dispatch of an expedition seemed to be justified on scientific grounds quite apart from the desire to obtain a high latitude.

When I found that some promises of support had failed me and had learned that the Royal Geographical Society, though sympathetic in its attitude, could not see its way to assist financially, I approached several gentlemen and suggested that they should guarantee me at the bank, the guarantees to be redeemed by me in 1910, after the return of the expedition. It was on this basis that I secured a sum of £20,000, the greater part of the money necessary for the starting of the expedition, and I cannot express too warmly my appreciation of the faith shown in me and my plans by the men who gave these guarantees, which could be redeemed only by the proceeds of lectures and the sale of my book after the expedition had concluded its work.*

FOODS TO PREVENT SCURVY

Several very important points have to be kept in view in selecting the food supplies for a polar expedition. In the first place, the food must be wholesome and nourishing in the highest degree possible. At one time that dread disease scurvy used to be regarded as the inevitable result of a prolonged stay in the ice-bound regions, and even the *Discovery* expedition, during its labors in the Antarctic in the years 1902–4, suffered from this complaint, which is often produced by eating preserved food that is not in a perfectly wholesome condition. It is now recognized that scurvy may be avoided if the closest attention is given to the preparation

*On his return from "Farthest South," the British government made Lieutenant Shackleton a grant of £20,000 to redeem these pledges.

and selection of foodstuffs along scientific lines, and I may say at once that our efforts in this direction were successful, for during the whole course of the expedition we had not one case of sickness attributable directly or indirectly to the foods we had brought with us. Indeed, beyond a few colds, apparently due to germs from a bale of blankets, we experienced no sickness at all at the winter quarters.

In the second place, the food taken for use on the sledging expeditions must be as light as possible, remembering always that extreme concentration renders the food less easy of assimilation, and therefore less healthful. Extracts that may be suitable enough for use in ordinary climates are of little use in the polar regions, because under conditions of very low temperature the heat of the body can be maintained only by use of fatty and farinaceous foods in fairly large quantities. Then the sledging foods must be such as do not require prolonged cooking—that is to say, it must be sufficient to bring them to the boiling point, for the amount of fuel that can be carried is limited. It must be possible to eat the foods without cooking at all, for the fuel may be lost or become exhausted.

Some important articles of food were presented to the expedition by the manufacturers, and others, such as biscuits and pemmican, were specially manufactured to my order. The question of packing presented some difficulties, and I finally decided to use "venesta" cases for the foodstuffs and as much as possible of the equipment. These cases are manufactured from composite boards prepared by uniting three layers of birch or other hard wood with waterproof cement. They are light, weather-proof, and strong, and proved to be eminently suited to our purposes. The cases I ordered measured about two feet six inches by fifteen inches, and we used about 2,500 of them. The saving of weight, as compared with an ordinary packing case, was about four pounds per case, and we had no trouble at all with breakages, in spite of the rough handling given our stores in the process of landing at Cape Royds after the expedition had reached the Antarctic regions.

FUR CLOTHING OF THE BEST

Our furs did not make a very large order, for after the experience of the *Discovery* expedition I decided to use fur only for the feet and hands and for the sleeping bags, relying for all other purposes on woolen garments with an outer covering of wind-proof materials. I ordered three large sleeping bags, to hold three men each, and twelve one-man bags. Each bag had the reindeer fur inside, and was lined with leather and specially strongly sewn.

The one-man bags weighed about ten pounds when dry, but of course the weight increased as they absorbed moisture when in use.

The foot-gear I ordered consisted of eighty pairs of ordinary finnesko, or reindeer fur boots, twelve pairs of special finnesko, and sixty pairs of ski boots of various sizes. The ordinary finnesko is made from the skin of the reindeer stag's head, with the fur outside, and its shape is roughly that of a very large boot without any laces. It is large enough to hold the foot, several pairs of socks, and a supply of sennegrass, and it is a wonderfully comfortable and warm form of foot-gear.

The special finnesko are made from the skin of the reindeer stag's legs, but they are not easily secured, for the reason that the native tribes, not unreasonably, desire to keep the best goods for themselves. I had a man sent to Lapland to barter for finnesko of the best kind, but he only succeeded in getting twelve pairs. The ski boots are made of soft leather, with the upper coming right round under the sole, and a flat piece of leather sewn on top of the upper. They are made specially for use with ski, and are very useful for summer wear. They give the foot plenty of play and do not admit water. The heel is very low, so that the foot can rest firmly on the ski. I bought five prepared reindeer skins for repairing and a supply of repairing gear, such as sinew, needles, and waxed thread.

GRASS USED IN THE SHOE TO PREVENT FREEZING

I have mentioned that sennegrass is used in the finnesko. This is dried grass of long fiber, with a special quality of absorbing moisture. I bought fifty kilos (109.37 pounds) in Norway for use on the expedition. The grass is sold in wisps, bound up tightly, and when the finnesko are being put on some of it is teased out and a pad placed along the sole under the foot. Then when the boot has been pulled on more grass is stuffed round the heel. The grass absorbs the moisture that is given off from the skin, and prevents the sock freezing to the sole of the boot, which would then be difficult to remove at night.

The grass is pulled out at night, shaken loose, and allowed to freeze. The moisture that has been collected congeals in the form of frost, and the greater part of it can be shaken away before the grass is replaced on the following morning. The grass is gradually used up on the march, and it is necessary to take a fairly large supply, but it is very light and takes up little room.

For use on the sledging expeditions I took six "Nansen" cookers made of aluminum, and of the pattern that has been adopted, with slight modifications, ever since Nansen made his famous journey in 1895–96. The sledging tents, of which I bought six, were made of light Willesden rot-proof drill, with a "spout" entrance of Burberry garberdine. They were green in color, as the shade is very restful to the eyes on the white snow plains, and weighed 27 pounds each, complete with five poles and floor cloth.

Each member of the expedition was supplied with two winter suits made of heavy blue pilot cloth, lined with Jaeger fleece. A suit consisted of a double-breasted jacket, vest and trousers, and weighed complete fourteen and three-quarter pounds.

An outer suit of wind-proof material is necessary in the polar regions, and I secured twenty-four suits of Burberry garberdine, each suit consisting of a short blouse, trouser overalls, and a helmet cover.

For use in the winter quarters we took four dozen Jaeger camel's-hair blankets and sixteen camel's-hair triple sleeping bags.

THE MANCHURIAN PONIES

I decided to take ponies, dogs, and a motor-car to assist in hauling our sledges on the long journeys that I had in view, but my hopes were based mainly on the ponies. Dogs had not proved satisfactory on the Barrier surface, and I did not expect my dogs to do as well as they actually did. The use of a motor-car was an experiment which I thought justified by my experience of the character of the Barrier surface, but I knew that it would not do to place much reliance on the machine in view of the uncertainty of the conditions. I felt confident, however, that the hardy ponies used in northern China and Manchuria would be useful if they could be landed on the ice in good condition.

I had seen these ponies in Shanghai, and I had heard of the good work they did on the Jackson-Harmsworth expedition. They are accustomed to hauling heavy loads in a very low temperature, and they are hardy, sure-footed, and plucky. I noticed that they had been used with success for very rough work during the Russo-Japanese war, and a friend who had lived in Siberia gave me some more information regarding their capabilities.

I therefore got into communication with the London manager of the Hongkong and Shanghai bank (Mr. C. S. Addis), and he was able to secure the services of a leading firm of veterinary surgeons in Shanghai. A qualified man went to Tientsin on my behalf, and from a mob of about two thousand of the ponies, brought down for sale from the northern regions, he selected fifteen of the little animals for my expedition.

The ponies chosen were all over twelve years and under seventeen years in age, and had spent the early part of their lives in the interior of Manchuria. They were practically unbroken, were about fourteen hands high, and were of various colors. They were all splendidly strong and healthy, full of tricks and wickedness, and ready for any amount of hard work over the snow-fields.

The fifteen ponies were taken to the coast and shipped by direct steamer to Australia. They came through the test of tropical temperatures unscathed, and at the end of October, 1907, arrived in Sydney, where they were met by Mr. Reid and at once transferred to a New Zealand bound steamer. The Colonial governments kindly consented to suspend the quarantine restrictions, which would have entailed exposure to summer heat for many weeks, and thirty-five days after leaving China

THE FOUR PONIES OUT FOR EXERCISE ON THE SEA ICE

the ponies were landed on Quail Island, in Port Lyttelton, and were free to scamper about and feed in idle luxury.

I had secured in London twenty tons of maize and ten hundredweight of compressed Maujee ration for the feeding of the ponies in the Antarctic. The maize was packed in about seven hundred tin-lined air-tight cases, and the ration was in one-pound air-tight tins. This ration consists of dried beef, carrots, milk, currants and sugar, and it provides a large amount of nourishment with comparatively little weight. One pound of the ration will absorb four pounds of water, and the ponies were very fond of it. We also secured in Australia ten tons of compressed fodder, consisting of oats, bran, and chaff. This fodder was packed in two hundred and fifty small bales.

I placed little reliance on the dogs, as I have already stated, but I thought it advisable to take some of these animals. I knew that a breeder in Stewart Island, New Zealand, had dogs descended from the Siberian dogs used on the Newnes-Borchgrevinck expedition, and I cabled to him to supply as many as he could up to forty. He was only able to let me have nine, but this team proved quite sufficient for the purposes of the expedition, as the arrival of pups brought the number up to twenty-two during the course of the work in the south.

THE SOUTH POLAR PARTY

Our party on leaving England consisted of:

E. H. Shackleton, commander.

Lieut. J. B. Adams, R. N. R., meteorologist.

Sir Philip Brocklehurst, Bart., assistant geologist and in charge of current observations.

Bernard Day, electrician and motor expert.

Ernest Joyce, in charge of general stores, dogs, sledges, and zoological collections.

Dr. A. F. Mackay, surgeon.

Dr. Eric Marshall, surgeon, cartographer.

G. E. Marston, artist.

James Murray, biologist.

Raymond Priestley, geologist.

William Roberts, cook.

Frank Wild, in charge of provisions.

Besides myself, Wild and Joyce only had had previous polar work, having been members of the *Discovery* expedition.

After the expedition had reached New Zealand and the generous assistance of the Australian and New Zealand governments had relieved me from some financial anxiety, I was able to add to the staff Douglas Mawson, lecturer of mineralogy and petrology at the Adelaide Uni-

MUSIC IN THE HUT DURING THE WINTER

DAY WITH THE MOTOR-CAR ON THE SEA ICE

versity, as physicist, and Bertram Armytage as a member of the expedition for general work; Prof. Edgeworth David, F. R. S., of Sydney University, as geologist and scientist; Leo Collon, a young Australian, and George Buckley, of New Zealand.

Our party found the hut which the *Discovery* party had abandoned at Cape Royds four years previously practically clear of snow, and the structure quite intact.

There was a small amount of ice inside on the walls, evidently the result of a summer thaw, but even after five years' desertion the building was in excellent preservation. A few relics of the last expedition were lying about,

including bags containing remnants of provisions from various sledging parties. Among these provisions was an open tin of tea, and the following morning the party made an excellent brew from the contents. It speaks volumes for the dryness of the climate that the tea should retain its flavor after exposure to the air for five years.

A sledging tin of petroleum was also used and was found to be in perfect condition. The ice on the end of Hut Point was cracked and crevassed, but in all other respects things seemed to be the same as when the *Discovery* steamed away to the north in February, 1904. The cross put up in memory of Vince, who lost

LANDING STORES FROM THE BOAT
AT THE FIRST LANDING PLACE AFTER THE ICE-FOOT HAD BROKEN AWAY

his life close by in a blizzard, was still standing, and so were the magnetic huts.

EXPERIENCES WITH THE PENGUINS

One day we were pulling along at a good rate, landing stores, when suddenly a heavy body shot out of the water, struck the seaman who was pulling stroke, and dropped with a thud into the bottom of the boat. The arrival was an Adelie penguin. It was hard to say who was the most astonished—the penguin, at the result of its leap on to what it had doubtless thought was a rock, or we, who so suddenly took on board this curious passenger. The sailors in the boat looked upon this incident as an omen of good luck. There is a tradition among seamen that the souls of old sailors, after death, occupy the bodies of penguins, as well as of albatrosses; this idea, however, does not prevent the mariners from making a hearty meal off the breasts of the penguins when opportunity offers.

The penguins were round us in large numbers. We had not had any time to make observations of them, being so busily employed discharging the ship, but just at this particular time our attention was called to a couple of these

DERRICK POINT,
SHOWING THE METHOD
OF HAULING STORES UP THE CLIFF

birds which suddenly made a spring from the water and landed on their feet on the ice-edge, having cleared a vertical height of twelve feet.

It seemed a marvelous jump for these small creatures to have made, and shows the rapidity with which they must move through the water to gain the impetus that enables them to clear a distance in vertical height four times greater than their own, and also how unerring must be their judgment in estimating the distance and height when performing this feat.

A blizzard interrupted the work of landing our supplies and buried everything under a thick mantle of snow.

The next four or five days were spent in using pick and shovel and iron crowbars on the envelope of ice that covered our cases, corners of which only peeped out from the mass. The whole had the appearance of a piece of the sweet known as almond rock, and there was as much difficulty in getting the cases clear of the ice as would be experienced if one tried to separate almonds from that sticky conglomerate without injury. Occasionally the breaking out of a case would disclose another which could be easily extracted, but more often each case required the pick or crowbars. A couple of earnest miners might be seen delving and hewing the ice off a case, of which only the corner could be seen, and after ten minutes' hard work it would be hauled up, and the stenciled mark of its contents exposed to view.

Brocklehurst took great interest in the recovery of the chocolate, and during this work took charge of one particular case which had been covered by the ice. He carried it himself up to the hut so as to be sure of its safety, and he was greeted with joy by the Professor, who recognized in the load some of his scientific instruments which were playing the part of the cuckoo in an old chocolate box. Needless to say Brocklehurst's joy was not as heartfelt as the Professor's.

THE WINTER HOUSE
BROUGHT FROM ENGLAND

Our winter headquarters was not a very spacious dwelling for the accommodation of fifteen persons, but our narrow quarters were warmer than if the hut had been larger.

The length inside was 33 feet, the breadth 19 feet, and the height to the eaves 8 feet. Between the outer wall and the inside lining of match-boarding, there was a space of about four inches, which was filled with granulated cork, serving to preserve the heat and keep out the cold. The outside was made of inch tongue-and-groove boarding, and a sloping roof, with a gable at each end and two ventilators, brought the total height up to 14 feet. The roof was double, but we did not fill the space between the two linings with cork, contenting ourselves with a double layer of felt over the outside roof, across which battens were nailed to protect the felt from the wind. While the felt was being nailed on, an Antarctic breeze came up, and some of the covering was stripped off. We found it hung up against rocks more than a mile away to the north, and eventually the work had to be done over again.

THE HUT IN THE EARLY WINTER

The building was made in England and shipped in sections all ready to be put together when the party landed. The hut was lit with acetylene gas.

The first thing done was to peg out a space for each individual, and we saw that the best plan would be to have the space allotted in sections, allowing two persons to share one cubicle. This space for two men amounted to six feet six inches in length and seven feet in depth from the wall of the hut towards the center. There were seven of these cubicles, and a space for the leader of the expedition; thus providing for the fifteen who made up the shore party.

THE PONIES GET SICK

It seems to be generally assumed that a Manchurian pony can drag a sledge over a broken trail at the rate of 20 to 30 miles a day, pulling not less than 1,200 pounds. Some authorities even put the weight to be hauled at 1,800 pounds, but this is, I think, far too heavy a load. It was a risk to take ponies from the far north through the tropics and then across 2,000 miles of stormy sea on a very small ship, but I had felt that if it could be done it would be well worth the trouble, for, compared with the dog, the pony is a far more efficient animal, one pony doing the work of at least ten dogs on the food allowance for ten dogs, and traveling a longer distance in a day.

We established ourselves at the winter quarters with eight ponies, but unfortunately we lost four of them within a month of our arrival. The loss was due, in the case of three of the four, to the fact that they were picketed when they first landed on sandy ground, and it was not noticed that they were eating the sand. I had neglected to see that the animals had a supply of salt given to them, and as they found a saline flavor in the volcanic sand under their feet, due to the fact that the blizzards had sprayed all the land near the shore with sea water, they ate it at odd moments.

All the ponies seem to have done this, but some were more addicted to the habit than the others. Several of them became ill, and we were quite at a loss to account for the trouble until Sandy died. Then a post-mortem examination revealed the fact that his stomach contained many pounds of sand, and the cause of the illness of the other ponies became apparent. We shifted them at once from the place where they were picketed, so that they could get no more sand, and gave them what remedial treatment lay in our power, but two more died in spite of all our efforts.

EREBUS, THE SENTINEL OF THE GREAT ICE BARRIER

On coming out of the hut one had only to go round the corner of the building in order to catch a glimpse of Mount Erebus, which lay directly behind us. Its summit was about fourteen miles from our winter quarters, but its slopes and foothills commenced within three-quarters of a mile of the hut.

Standing as a sentinel at the gate of the Great Ice Barrier, Erebus forms a magnificent picture. The great mountain rises from sea-level to an altitude of over 13,000 feet, looking out across the Barrier, with its enormous snow-clad bulk towering above the white slopes that run up from the coast. At the top of the mountain an immense depression marks the site of the old crater, and from the side of this rises the active cone, generally marked by steam or smoke. The ascent of such a mountain would be a matter of difficulty in any part of the world, hardly to be attempted without experienced guides, but the difficulties were accentuated by the latitude of Erebus.

The observer taking the meteorological observations every two hours had the mountain in sight, and as Erebus was our high-level mete-orological observatory, to the crown of which we always looked for indications of wind-currents at that elevation, we naturally saw every phase of activity produced by the fires within. It was for this reason, no doubt, that during the period of our stay in these regions, more especially through the winter months, we were able to record a fairly constant condition of activity on the mountain. It became quite an ordinary thing to hear reports from men who had been outside during the winter that there was a "strong glow on Erebus." These glows at times were much more vivid than at others. On one particular occasion, when the barometer showed a period of extreme depression, the glow was much more active, waxing and waning at intervals of a quarter of an hour through the night, and at other times we have seen great bursts of flame crowning the crater.

The huge steam column that rises from the crater into the cold air shot up at times to a height of 3,000 or 4,000 feet before spreading out and receiving its line direction from the air-currents at that particular hour holding the upper atmosphere. There were occasions when the view of this steam cloud became much more vivid, and we found that the best view that could be obtained was when the moon, rising in the eastern sky, passed behind the summit of the mountain. Then, projected on the disc of the moon, we could see the great cloud traveling upward, not quietly, but impelled by force from below.

There were times also when it was obvious that the molten lava in the crater could not have been very far from the lip of the cup, for we could see the deep-red glow reflected strongly on the steam cloud. We often speculated as to the course the lava stream would take and its probable effect on the great glaciers and snow-fields flanking the sides of the mountain, should it ever overflow. These sudden uprushes were obviously the result of a vast steam explosion in the interior of the volcano and were sufficient proofs that Erebus still possesses considerable activity.

THE ASCENT OF EREBUS

Before the winter set in, several members of the party climbed to the summit of Erebus. Their achievement will rank high among mountain climbs, for the party was compelled to endure temperatures of below zero, to fight through raging blizzards, and often the ascent was so steep as to be nearly insurmountable. From the summit they could look down into the fiery chasm of the volcano.

"We stood on the verge of a vast abyss, and at first could see neither to the bottom nor across it on account of the huge mass of steam filling the crater and soaring aloft in a column 500 to 1,000 feet high. After a continuous loud hissing sound, lasting for some minutes, there would come from below a big dull boom, and immediately great globular masses of steam would rush upward to swell the volume of the snow-white cloud which ever sways over the crater. This phenomenon recurred at intervals during the whole of our stay at the crater. Meanwhile, the air around us was extremely redolent of burning sulphur. Presently a pleasant northerly breeze fanned away the steam cloud, and at once the whole crater stood revealed to us in all its vast extent and depth.

"Mawson's angular measurement made the depth 900 feet and the greatest width about half a mile. There were at least three well-defined openings at the bottom of the cauldron, and it was from these that the steam explosions pro-

THE CAMP 7,000 FEET UP MOUNT EREBUS:
THE STEAM FROM THE ACTIVE CRATER CAN BE SEEN

ceeded. Near the southwest portion of the crater there was an immense rib in the rim, perhaps 300 to 400 feet deep. The crater wall opposite the one at the top of which we were standing presented features of special interest. Beds of dark pumiceous lava or pumice alternated with white zones of snow. There was no direct evidence that the snow was bedded with the lava, though it was possible that such may have been the case. From the top of one of the thickest of the lava or pumice beds, just where it touched the belt of snow, there rose scores of small steam jets all in a row. They were too numerous and too close together to have been each an independent fumarole; the appearance was rather suggestive of the snow being converted into steam by the heat of the layer of rock immediately below it."

Two features of the geology of Erebus which are specially distinctive are the vast quantities of large and perfect feldspar crystals and the ice fumaroles. The crystals are from two to three inches in length. Many of them have had their angles and edges slightly rounded by attrition, through clashing against one another when they were originally projected from the funnel of the volcano, but numbers of them are beautifully perfect. The fluid lava which once surrounded them has been blown away in the form of fine dust by the force of steam explosions, and the crystals have been left behind intact.

The ice fumaroles are specially remarkable. About fifty of these were visible to us on the track which we followed to and from the crater, and doubtless there were numbers that we did not see. These unique ice-mounds have resulted from the condensation of vapor around the orifices of the fumaroles. It is only under conditions of very low temperature that such structures could exist. No structures like them are known in any other part of the world.

LIFE DISCOVERED IN THE ICE DURING THE WINTER

On March 13 we experienced a very fierce blizzard. The hut shook and rocked in spite of our sheltered position, and articles that we had left lying loose outside were scattered far and wide. Even cases weighing from 50 to 80 pounds were shifted from where they had been resting, showing the enormous velocity of the wind. When the gale was over we put everything that was likely to blow away into positions of greater safety.

It was on this day also that Murray found living microscopical animals on some fungus that had been thawed out from a lump of ice taken from the bottom of one of the lakes. This was one of the most interesting biological discoveries that had been made in the Antarctic, for the study of these minute creatures occupied our biologist for a great part of his stay in the south, and threw a new light on the capability of life to exist under conditions of extreme cold and in the face of great variations of temperature.

We all became vastly interested in the rotifers during our stay, and the work of the biologist in this respect was watched with keen attention. From our point of view there was an element of humor in the endeavors of Murray to slay the little animals he had found. He used to thaw them out from a block of ice, freeze them up again, and repeat this process several times without producing any result as far as the rotifers were concerned. Then he tested them in brine so strongly saline that it would not freeze at a temperature above minus 7° Fahr., and still the animals lived. A good proportion of them survived a temperature of 200° Fahr. It became a contest between rotifers and scientist, and generally the rotifers seemed to triumph.

THE SOUTHERN PARTY

The southern party, consisting of Shackleton, Adams, Marshall, and Wild, left the winter quarters October 29, 1908, and for five weeks headed up the Ice Barrier.

On November 26 we camped in latitude 82° 18½′ south, longitude 168° east, having passed the "furthest south" record. New land had come within our range of vision by this time, owing to the fact that we were far out from the base of the mountains, and I had noted with some anxiety that the coast trended south-southeast, thus threatening to cross our path and obstruct the way to the pole. We could see great snow-clad mountains rising beyond Mount Longstaff, and also far inland to the north of Mount Markham. On November 26 we opened out Shackleton Inlet, and looking up it sighted a great chain of mountains, while to the west of Cape Wilson appeared another chain of sharp

THE CRATER OF EREBUS, 900 FEET DEEP AND HALF A MILE WIDE:
STEAM IS SEEN RISING ON THE LEFT

The photograph was taken from the lower part of the crater edge.

A REMARKABLE FUMAROLE IN THE OLD CRATER, IN THE FORM OF A COUCHANT LION:
THE MEN (FROM THE LEFT) ARE: MACKAY, DAVID, ADAMS, MARSHALL

peaks, about 10,000 feet high, stretching away to the north beyond Snow Cape, and continuing the land on which Mount A. Markham lies.

The first pony had been killed on November 21, when we were south of the 81st parallel, and we had left a depot of pony meat and ordinary stores, to provide for the return march. We started at once to use pony meat as part of the daily ration, and soon found that scraps of raw, frozen meat were of assistance on the march in maintaining our strength and cooling our parched throats. A second pony was shot on November 28, and a third on December 1, by which time we were closing in on the land, and

it had become apparent that we would have to find a way over the mountains if we were to continue the southern march.

We were still sighting new land ahead, and the coast line had a more distinct easterly trend. We camped on December 2 in latitude 83° 28′ south, longitude 171° 30′ east, opposite a red granite mountain about 3,000 feet in height. On the following day we climbed this mountain, and from its summit saw an enormous glacier, stretching almost due south, flanked by huge mountains, and issuing on to the Barrier south of our camp. We decided at once that we had better ascend the glacier, and on the following day made our way, with two sledges and the last pony, on to its surface.

ASCENDING A GLACIER
WHICH WAS 130 MILES IN LENGTH

We encountered difficulties at once, for the snow-slopes by means of which we gained the glacier surface gave way to blue ice, with numberless cracks and crevasses, many of them razor-edged. Traveling on this surface in finnesko was slow and painful work.

On December 5 Marshall and Adams, who were ahead looking for a route, reported that at a point close to the granite cliffs a bird, brown in color, with a white line under each wing, had flown over their heads. They were sure it was not a skua gull, the only bird likely to have been attracted by the last dead pony. It was a curious incident to occur in latitude 83° 40′ south. We left the fourth depot close to the foot of the glacier at the foot of a wonderful granite cliff, polished by the winds and snows of ages. On December 6 we took six hours to pass about 600 yards of severely crevassed ice, over which all our gear had to be relayed, and on the following day we lost the last pony, which fell into a crevasse disguised, like so many others, by a treacherous snow-lid. Wild was leading the pony with one sledge, while Adams, Marshall, and myself went on ahead with the other sledge and pioneered a practical path. We had passed over a snow-covered crevasse without noticing it, but the greater weight of the pony broke through the lid, and the animal dropped through, probably to a depth of several hundreds of feet. Happily the swingle-tree snapped with a sudden strain, and Wild and the sledge were saved. This accident left us with two sledges and a weight of about 250 pounds per

man to haul. Our altitude at this time was about 1,700 feet above sea-level.

During the days that followed we made steady progress up the glacier, experiencing constant difficulty with the crevasses. We hauled well ahead of the sledges, so that when one of us dropped through a snow-lid the harness would support him until he could be hauled up again. We had many painful falls as a result of having no footgear suitable for the ice-climbing, and any future travelers would do well to take boots with spikes. A special form would have to be devised, on account of the low temperature rendering impracticable the use of ordinary mountaineering boots.

COAL AND FOSSIL WOOD DISCOVERED

New land appeared day after day, and we were able to make small geological collections and to take some photographs. The rocks were sedimentary, the lines of stratification often showing clearly on the mountain sides, and we made two geological discoveries of the first importance. In latitude 85° south, Wild, who had climbed the slope of a mountain in order to look ahead, found coal, six seams ranging from 4 inches to 7 or 8 feet in thickness, with sandstone intervening. Close to this point I found a piece of sandstone showing an impression, and microscopic investigation has shown that this was fossil coniferous wood.

The glacier proved to be about 130 miles in length, rising to an altitude of over 9,000 feet. Christmas day, 1908, found us in latitude 85° 55′ south, a plateau with ice-falls appearing to the south. Much glaciated land trended to the southeast, apparently ending in a high mountain shaped like a keep. The land to the west had been left behind. It was evident that we were still below the plateau level, and, though

SKUA GULLS FEEDING NEAR THE HUT AT CAPE ROYDS

we were getting free of crevasses, we were hindered by much soft snow. The level was rising in a series of steep ridges about 7 miles apart. We had started to reduce rations before leaving the Barrier surface, and by Christmas day were marching on very short commons. Our temperature was 2° subnormal, but otherwise we were well and fit.

On December 31 we camped in latitude 86° 54′ south. We had not yet reached the plateau level, for slopes still lay ahead, and our altitude was about 10,000 feet. We had three weeks' food on a reduced ration, and were 186 geo-graphical miles from the pole. The land had been left behind, and we were traveling over a white expanse of snow, still with rising slopes ahead. We were weakening from the combined effects of short food, low temperature, high altitude, and heavy work. We were able to march on the first six days of January, and on the night of January 6 camped in latitude 88° 7′ south. We had increased the daily ration, for it had become evident that vitality could not be maintained on the amount of food we had been taking. I had been forced to abandon the hope of reaching the pole, and we were concentrating our efforts on getting within 100 miles of the goal.

CAUGHT IN A BLIZZARD

A fierce blizzard blew on January 7 and 8, and made any march impossible. We lay in our sleeping bags, frequently attacked by frost-bite. The following paragraphs are quoted from my diary.

"January 7.—A blinding, shrieking blizzard all day, with the temperature ranging from 60° to 70° of frost. It has been impossible to leave the tent, which is snowed up on the lee side. We have been lying in our bags all day, only warm at food time, with fine snow making through the walls of the worn tent and covering our bags. We are greatly cramped. Adams is suffering from cramp every now and then. We are eating our valuable food without marching.

The wind has been blowing 80 to 90 miles an hour. We can hardly sleep. Tomorrow I trust this will be over. Directly the wind drops we march as far south as possible, then plant the flag and turn homeward. Our chief anxiety is that our tracks may drift up, for to them we must trust mainly to find our depot; we have no land bearings in this great plain of snow. It is a serious risk that we have taken, but we had to play the game to the utmost, and Providence will look after us.

January 8.—Again all day in our bags, suffering considerably physically from cold hands and feet and from hunger, but more mentally, for we cannot get on south, and we simply lie here shivering. Every now and then one of our party's feet go, and the unfortunate beggar has to take his leg out of the sleeping bag and have his frozen foot nursed into life again by placing it inside the shirt, against the skin, of his almost equally unfortunate neighbor.

We must do something more to the south, even though the food is going, and we weaken lying in the cold, for with 72° of frost the wind cuts through our thin tent, and even the drift is finding its way in and on to our bags, which are wet enough as it is. Cramp is not uncommon every now and then, and the drift all round the tent has made it so small that there is hardly room for us at all. The wind has been blowing hard all day; some of the gusts must be over 70 or 80 miles an hour.

This evening it seems as though it were going to ease down, and directly it does we shall be up and away south for a rush. I feel that this march must be our limit. We are so short of food, and at this high altitude, 11,600 feet, it is hard to keep any warmth in our bodies between the scanty meals. We have nothing to read now, having depoted our little books to save weight, and it is dreary work lying in the tent with nothing to read, and too cold to write much in the diary.

110 MILES FROM THE SOUTH POLE

January 9.—Our last day outward. We have shot our bolt, and the tale is latitude 88° 23′ south, longitude 162° east. The wind eased down at 1 a.m., and at 2 a.m. we were up and had breakfast. At 4 a.m. we started south, with the Queen's Union Jack, a brass cylinder containing stamps and documents to place at the farthest south point, camera, glasses, and compass. At 9 a.m. we were in 88° 23′ south, half running and half walking over a surface much hardened by the recent blizzard. It was strange for us to go along without the nightmare of a sledge dragging behind us.

We hoisted her Majesty's flag and the other Union Jack afterwards, and took possession of the plateau in the name of his Majesty. While the Union Jack blew out stiffly in the icy gale that cut us to the bone, we looked south with our powerful glasses, but could see nothing but the dead white snow plain. There was no break in the plateau as it extended toward the pole, and we feel sure that the goal we have failed to reach lies on this plain.

We stayed only a few minutes, and then, taking the Queen's flag and eating our scanty meal as we went, we hurried back and reached our camp about 3 p. m. We were so dead tired that we only did an hour's march in the afternoon and camped at 5 p. m. The temperature was minus 19° Fahr. Fortunately for us, our tracks were not obliterated by the blizzard; indeed, they stood up, making a trail easily followed. Homeward bound at last. Whatever regrets may be, we have done our best."

THE HOMEWARD MARCH

The homeward march was rendered difficult by shortage of food and attacks of dysentery due to the meat from one of the ponies.

We had a strong wind behind us day after day during this period, and this contributed in a very large measure to our safety, for in the weakened condition we had then reached we could not have made long marches against a head wind, and without long marches we would have starved between the depots. We had a sail on the sledge, formed of the floor cloth of a tent, and often the sledge would overrun us, though at other times it would catch in a drift and throw us heavily.

The results of the southern journey may be summarized briefly. We found that a chain of great mountains stretched north by east from Mount Markham as far as the 86th parallel, and that other ranges ran toward the southwest, south, and southeast between the 84th and the 86th parallels. We ascended one of the largest glaciers in the world on to a high plateau, which in all probability is a continuation of the Victoria Land plateau. The geographical pole almost certainly lies on this plateau, at an altitude of between 10,000 and 11,000 feet above sea-level. The discovery of coal and fossil wood has a very important bearing on the question of the past geological history of the Antarctic continent.

FROSTBITE AND SUNBURN AT THE SAME TIME

When we were traveling along during the early part of the journey over the level Barrier surface, we felt the heat of the sun severely, though as a matter of fact the temperature was generally very low, sometimes as low as zero Fahr., though the season was the height of summer. It was quite usual to feel one side of the face getting frozen while the other side was being sunburned. The ponies would have frozen perspiration on their coats on the sheltered side, while the sun would keep the other side hot and dry, and as the day wore on and the sun moved round the sky the frosted area on the animals would change its position in sympathy.

I remember that on December 4 we were marching stripped to our shirts, and we got very much sunburned, though at noon that day the air temperature showed ten degrees of frost. When we started to climb the glacier and marched close to the rocks, we felt the heat much more, for the rocks acted as radiators, and this experience weighed with me in deciding to leave all the spare clothing and equipment at the Upper Glacier depot, about 7,000 feet up. We did not expect to have to climb much higher, but we did not reach the plateau until we had climbed over 10,000 feet above sea-level, and so we felt the cold extremely. Our wind-proof Burberry clothing had become thin by this time, and had been patched in many places in consequence of having been torn on the sharp ice.

The wind got in through a tear in my Burberry trousers one day and I was frost-bitten on the under part of the knee. This frost-bite developed into an open wound, into which the wool from my underclothing worked, and I had finally to perform a rather painful operation with a knife before the wound would heal. We were continually being frost-bitten up on the plateau, and when our boots had begun to give out and we were practically marching on

the sennegrass inside the finnesko our heels got frost-bitten. My heels burst when we got on to hard stuff, and for some time my socks were caked with blood at the end of every day's march. Finally Marshall put some "newskin" on a pad, and that stuck on well until the cracks had healed. The scars are likely to remain with me.

In the very cold days, when our strength had begun to decrease, we found great difficulty in hoisting the sail on our sledge, for when we lifted our arms above our heads in order to adjust the sail the blood ran from our fingers and they promptly froze. Ten minutes or a

AN ICE CAVE IN THE WINTER

ICE FLOWERS ON NEWLY FORMED SEA ICE EARLY IN THE WINTER

quarter of an hour sometimes elapsed before we could get the sledge properly rigged. Our troubles with frost-bite were no doubt due in a measure to the lightness of our clothing, but there was compensation in the speed with which we were able to travel. I have no doubt at all that men engaged in polar exploration should be clothed as lightly as is possible, even if there is a danger of frost-bite when they halt on the march.

We would certainly not have traveled so fast had we been wearing the regulation pilot-cloth garment generally used in polar explora-tion. Our experience made it obvious that a party which hopes to reach the pole must take more food per man than we did, but how the additional weight is to be provided for is a mat-ter of individual consideration. I would not take cheese again, for although it is a good food, we did not find it as palatable as chocolate, which is practically as sustaining. Our other foods were all entirely satisfactory.

THE DIVISION OF WORK

Each member of the southern party had his own particular duties to perform. Adams had charge of the meteorology, and his work involved the taking of temperatures at regular intervals, and the boiling of the hypsometer, sometimes several times in a day. He took notes during the day, and wrote up the observations at night in the sleeping bag. Marshall was the cosmographer and took the angles and bearings of all the new land; he also took the meridian altitudes and the compass variations as we went south. When a meridian altitude was taken, I generally had it checked by each member of the party, so that the mean could be taken.

Marshall's work was about the most uncomfortable possible, for at the end of a day's march, and often at lunch-time, he would have to stand in the biting wind handling the screws of the theodolite. The map of the journey was prepared by Marshall, who also took most of the photographs. Wild attended to the repair of the sledges and equipment, and also assisted me in the geological observations and the collection of specimens. It was he who found the coal close to the Upper Glacier depot. I kept the courses and distances, worked out observations, and laid down our directions. We all kept diaries. I had two, one my observation book and the other the narrative diary, reproduced in the first volume.

To the biologist, no more uninviting desert is imaginable than Cape Royds seemed when we made our first landing, and for long afterwards. Here is absolute desolation, a black and white wilderness, rugged ridges of lava alternating with snowdrifts for a few miles, ending to the north and south in crevassed glaciers, and eastward in the snow-field stretching up to the rocky crags of the cone of Mount Erebus.

On the very edge of the sea, the little colony of Adelie penguins and the scattered skua gulls relieved the monotony. Beyond was no living creature, no blade of grass, or tiniest patch of welcome green.

Bleak and bare though it was, this stretch of two or three miles of broken country, where rocky peaks and ridges, moraines and snow drifts diversified the surface, was the field of operations for the biologist. The white waste of glacier and snow-field was hopeless; the nearer country seemed little more promising.

The sea was there known to be teeming with varied life, but it was inaccessible till the ice should bridge it over.

Water-bears were found to live while frozen in ice just as well as the rotifers did. It is an interesting fact that the only abundant species at Cape Royds is an Arctic species (*Macrobiotus arcticus*) which was only previously known in Spitzbergen and Franz Josef Land, and which has not yet been detected in the various collections made on the other side of the Antarctic by Bruce's and Nordenskjold's expeditions.

The mystery of the Great Ice Barrier has not been solved, and it would seem that the question of its formation and extent cannot be determined definitely until an expedition traces the line of the mountains round its southerly edge. A certain amount of light has been thrown on the construction of the Barrier, in that we were able, from observations and measurements, to conclude provisionally that it is composed mainly of snow. The Barrier still continues its recession, which has been observed since the voyage of Sir James Ross in 1842. There certainly appears to be a high snow-covered land on the 163d meridian, where we saw slopes and peaks, entirely snow covered, rising to a height of 800 feet, but we did not see any bare rocks, and did not have an opportunity to take soundings at this spot. We could not arrive at any definite conclusion on the point.

The journey made by the northern party resulted in the attainment of the South Magnetic Pole, the position of which was fixed, by observations made on the spot and in the neighborhood, at latitude 72° 25′ south, longitude 155° 16′ east. The first part of this journey was made along the coast-line of Victoria Land, and many new peaks, glaciers and ice-tongues were discovered, in addition to a couple of small islands. The whole of the coast traversed was carefully triangulated, and the existing map was corrected in several respects.

THE SOUTH POLAR EXPEDITION

To the Members of the National Geographic Society:

ON February 1 Commander Robert E. Peary made a proposition to the Board of Managers of the National Geographic Society that the Society and the Peary Arctic Club should together send out an expedition to the South Polar regions to explore the coast of Weddell Sea and, if possible, reach the South Pole via this route. The proposed expedition would leave the United States in August of this year and cross the Antarctic circle about January 1, 1911. Commander Peary offered on behalf of the Peary Arctic Club to place the steamship *Roosevelt*, which it will be remembered was built by the Club specially for polar work, at the disposal of the expedition, provided the Society would assume the initial expense of $50,000. He also proposed that expenses above $50,000 be divided equally between the Peary Arctic Club and the National Geographic Society. He estimates the total expense of fitting out and maintaining an expedition in the South Polar regions for one year at between $75,000 and $100,000.

Commander Peary stated, moreover, that the *Roosevelt* was in very good condition; that she could not be duplicated at present for considerably over $100,000, and that all the equipment of his recent polar expedition, including sledges, fur clothing, and camp equipment, would be placed at the disposal of the party, and that if funds could be found for the expedition Captain Bartlett and the major portion of the members and crew of his last expedition, who were of such invaluable assistance to him in his conquest of the pole, would be glad to take part in the work. He himself was ready to devote his time and energy to planning and equipping the expedition, but could not take command of the party. Captain Bartlett will command the expedition.

Your Board of Managers agreed with Commander Peary that the present is a most opportune time for an American expedition to the Antarctic. A British expedition under Captain Scott will leave England about August, 1910, and spend the year of 1911 in Victoria Land and will attempt to reach the South Pole from that quarter. Simultaneous observations taken by an American party exactly opposite the English base would be of great benefit to science.

Your Board of Managers referred the matter for consideration to the Finance and Research Committees of the Society. On February 8 favorable reports from these two committees were received by the Society. The following resolution was thereupon unanimously adopted by the Board:

"*Resolved:* The National Geographic Society believes that it is of great importance to science that tidal, magnetic, and meteorological observations shall be obtained at or in the vicinity of Coats Land during the same period that the British expedition under Captain Robert F. Scott, R. N., is making similar observations on the other side of the Antarctic area, 1,800 miles distant, and at the same time that this recently discovered land shall be explored.

"The Society is ready to accept Commander Peary's proposition that it shall undertake jointly with the Peary Arctic Club an expedition to the Antarctic regions, provided that the Board of Managers, after consultation with the members of the Society, finds that the project will receive sufficient financial assistance to warrant the undertaking."

The Board of Managers heartily endorse Commander Peary's project, and, if the resources of the Society were larger, would make an appropriation for the work. All our funds, however, are required at home.

The membership and popularity of the National Geographic Society have been increasing so rapidly that the Association requires additional space for its working force. During the past year the Society has expended about $40,000 in purchasing a frontage of 85 feet on Sixteenth street, with a depth of 90 feet, adjoining its present home. Your Board of Managers propose on this site to erect an additional build-ing which will afford room for the clerical force of the Society and for the future growth of its business. This expenditure will require all of the available funds of the Society.

We realize, however, the unusual opportunity afforded the National Geographic Society by Commander Robert E. Peary for the increase of geographic knowledge of the South Polar regions. We believe not only that the members of the Society should be given an opportunity, but that they should be urged to assist the project.

An American expedition could be equipped at the present time with great economy of money, could benefit by Commander Peary's unequaled experience of polar conditions, and could use the officers and crew picked and trained by him during many years of campaigns on the ice.

As Peary says, "At some sacrifice and cost of time and money on my part, and large cost of money on the part of my friends, a certain capital of experience and equipment has been assembled which has no duplicate, and I feel that it is perhaps a duty not to let that capital be thrown away when a little further expenditure of time and effort will enable it to bring in still greater returns."

As evidence of his desire to see an American expedition despatched in search of the South Pole, Commander Peary has deposited $10,000 in a New York bank as his subscription to such an expedition. This sum had been presented him by Governor Hughes on behalf of the American people February 8 at a large meeting in the Metropolitan Opera House.

No region in the world presents such problems for exploration and the advancement of science as are to be found around the South Pole. Here is a continent greater than the United

States and Alaska combined, much larger than Europe, which has been penetrated in only one direction, namely, by Scott and Shackleton from Victoria Land. Even its coast lines are little known. It is believed that the greater part of this continent ranges in altitude from 8,000 to 14,000 feet above the sea, making it probably the largest continental mass above sea-level in the world.

Planted on the fringe of this vast continent of snow and ice are lofty volcanoes like Terror and Erebus, which are belching continually smoke and fire. Here lives the most remarkable bird known to science, the penguin, which lays its egg on a cake of ice in the blackness of a polar night, when the temperature is not less than 30° below zero, and then holds the egg and chick on its feet until the young bird can take care of itself.

A glance at the map (page 92) shows the dense pack ice which surrounds the Antarctic area and makes the approach to land so difficult from all directions. But the great engines and heavy frame of the *Roosevelt*, which is more powerful than any vessel hitherto employed in South Polar work, should enable her to pound a path where previous ships have been helpless, and thus to carry the American party to an advantageous base. Exactly where this base shall be cannot be determined until the party get in the ice and find where they can go, but Commander Peary proposes that the American expedition should make its headquarters somewhere on the coast of Weddell Sea, probably in the vicinity of Coats Land, which was discovered by Captain Bruce, of the Scottish expedition, in 1904. It is hoped that a base can be found here less than 900 miles from the pole. The primary object of the expedition would be to plant the Stars and Stripes at the South Pole, but for those who seek a different motive, it should be explained that every mile made from Coats Land to the pole would be over unpenetrated and unknown regions.

This section is probably the least known in the Antarctic area. Bruce succeeded in getting within a few miles of the coast, but he did not land. Ahead of him were ice-clad slopes which he believes ascend to a plateau which may be an extension of Victoria Land. All explorations in this region would be absolutely new discoveries and would benefit geology, zoology, and all kindred sciences.

If the plan of exploration outlined above is put into successful execution we hope it will arouse such interest that our government or an association of scientific organizations, or both in combination, will later undertake the exploration and scientific investigation of the entire circuit of the unknown Antarctic regions, including the exploration of Wilkes Land and the verification of discoveries made 70 years ago.

Campaigning against the pole in some respects is easier in the South than in the North. The weather is much harsher and more boisterous in the South, but the working season is longer. The North Pole is surrounded by an ice-covered ocean, which must be crossed in spring, before the ice breaks apart under the summer sun. The South Pole, on the other hand, is situated on a great ice plateau, which may be traversed during almost the entire period of daylight. Thus, while Peary was compelled to complete his dash from the most northern land to the pole and back in a period of less than 60 days, the South Polar explorer has more than 120 days at his disposal, and even this period can be extended by utilizing Peary's methods and equipment.

WILKES' AND D'URVILLE'S DISCOVERIES IN WILKES LAND

By Rear Admiral John E. Pillsbury, U. S. Navy

IN January, 1840, two national expeditions were in the Antarctic, one the United States Exploring Expedition, consisting of four ships, the *Vincennes*, *Peacock*, *Porpoise*, and *Flying Fish*, under the command of Lieut. Charles Wilkes, U. S. Navy, and the other a French expedition, consisting of *L'Astrolabe* and *La Zélée*, under command of Capitaine de Vaisseau M. J. Dumont d'Urville.

It has generally been accepted by foreign authorities that d'Urville sighted the land of the Antarctic Continent, which he named Adélie Land, on the same day (January 19) that Wilkes discovered land 400 miles to the eastward, which he named Cape Hudson, and also that d'Urville's Cote Clarie, in longitude 131° east, was sighted by him the day before it was seen by Lieutenant Ringgold, on board U. S. S. *Porpoise*.

Investigation shows that both of these assumptions are in error, and in fact d'Urville first sighted Adélie Land the day after Wilkes sighted Cape Hudson, and he sighted Cote Clarie the

same day that it was sighted by Ringgold, but at a later hour. The story of the investigation which led to these conclusions will be given in the order in which it was made.

In d'Urville's narrative it is stated under date of *January 29* that at 4 p. m. he sighted one of the ships of the American expedition (the *Porpoise*) and he "hoped that she intended to speak us." Through a misunderstanding of the maneuvering of the French flag-ship, Ringgold thought d'Urville wished to avoid a meeting, and, although but "a cable's length distant" from the ship, he put his helm up and stood off to the southward.

Ringgold states that at 4 p. m. *January 30* he sighted two ships which afterwards proved to be the French vessels. He approached them "within musket shot," when to his surprise he saw them making sail, whereupon he hauled down his colors and stood off before the wind.

The discrepancy in dates was not noticed in reading the narratives, but, wishing to see just where the meeting of the ships took place, their tracks were plotted on the same chart, when it appeared that the noon positions (d'Urville's January 29 and Ringgold's January 30) were near each other, and that the tracks crossed in the afternoon.

The discrepancy in dates seems to be remarkable, since both expeditions had crossed the 180th meridian from east to west some months before and had sailed for the Antarctic—one from Hobart Town, Tasmania, and the other from Sydney, Australia, where the dates must have been identical.

We find in Wilkes' narrative, volume 2, page 159, this statement: "On crossing the meridian 180° we dropped the 14th of November, in order to make our time correspond to that of the Eastern Hemisphere, to which our operations were for some months to be confined."

That d'Urville made no change of date in crossing the 180th meridian, but maintained the same chronology, appears from d'Urville's narrative, "Routes des Corvettes," volume I, page 134, where, under date of October 13, 1838, the longitude is given as 179° 31′ west, and on page 136, under date of October 14, 1838, it is given as 178° 53′ east. He therefore made no change of date in crossing the 180th meridian, as otherwise the second date would have been October 15 instead of October 14.

Further investigation of d'Urville's daily positions shows that every day is accounted for until June 22, 1840, which appears in volume 1, page 340. On page 342 appears the date of June 24, with an asterisk, and at the bottom of the page is this note:

"Nous reprenons la date d'Europe,"

so that the date he dropped was June 23, 1840, five months after the visit to the Antarctic and more than twenty months since he crossed the 180th meridian.

This means that in d'Urville's narrative of his discoveries and on the chart of his Antarctic voyage every noon position must have its date advanced one day in any comparison to be made with the noon positions and the discoveries of Wilkes' ships.

Wilkes believed that he sighted the Antarctic Continent on January 16, 1840, at about 158° east longitude. On January 19, however, he states that land was now certainly visible from the *Vincennes*, both to the south-southeast and southwest, in the former direction most distinctly. Both appeared high," etc.

D'Urville says, in volume 8 of his narrative, under date of January 19 (which should be January 20, to correspond with Wilkes' time), "At 9 a. m. we saw in the E. S. E. a great black cloud, which seemed stationary and had the appearance of a raised island." "Toward 3 p. m., M. Gervaize, who was officer of the watch, thought he saw once more an indication of land in the east." "At 10:50 p. m. this luminary (the sun) disappeared and showed up the raised contour of the land in all its sharpness." This land on January 21 (true date, 22) he named Adélie Land.

Returning now to the meeting of the *Porpoise* and the French vessels. On the day following the meeting d'Urville reports: "At 6 o'clock the man on lookout had sighted the ice pack to the south and I brought the ship to the wind in order to go nearer to explore it. At 10 o'clock we were not more than three or four miles distant. It appeared prodigious. We saw a cliff with a uniform height of 100 to 150 feet, forming a long line westward," etc.

It will be noticed that at 6 o'clock the *ice pack* and not the *barrier* was sighted.

Wilkes' narrative of the movements of the *Porpoise* for this day states: "The beginning of the 31st the gale continued; at 7 a. m., moderating, they again made sail to the westward; in half an hour discovered a high barrier of ice to the northward, with ice islands to the southward; at 10 a. m. they found themselves in a great inlet formed of vast fields of ice which they had entered twelve hours previously; the only opening appearing to the eastward, they were compelled to retrace their steps, which was effected by 8 p. m." "They now found themselves out of this dangerous position, and, passing the point, kept away to the westward."

"February 1.—The immense perpendicular barrier encountered yesterday was now in sight trending as far as the eye could reach to the westward," etc.

The *Porpoise*, therefore, at 7:30 a. m., January 31, was in the entrance of the great inlet on the southeast side of d'Urville's "Cote Clarie," and had sighted the high barrier of ice, the northern side of which d'Urville reached about 10 o'clock the same forenoon.

It is established from this investigation that, even if Wilkes' sighting the Antarctic Continent on January 16 is not admitted, it is certain that he did sight Cape Hudson a day before d'Urville sighted Adélie Land, and that Cote Clarie was sighted by the *Porpoise* on the same day that it was seen by d'Urville, but at an earlier hour.

Wilkes cruised along the coast of this continent for more than 1,600 miles from his first landfall. Future exploration may, and, indeed, probably will, find that much of the land discovered by him was placed too near the barrier, or, in other words, too far north, for it is well known that distance estimated by the eye is liable to great error, and particularly is this the case in the polar regions.

Whether this proves to be so or not, this investigation establishes Wilkes' priority over d'Urville. The English sealer Balleny, in 1839, got a glimpse of land in about 121° east, but all he says regarding it is, "Saw land to the southward." Neither d'Urville nor Balleny had any notion nor made any suggestion that they were on the edge of a continent. Wilkes, on the contrary, not only sighted at frequent intervals some 1,600 miles of this coast, but he recognized that it must be part of a continent. The name he gave to this land, the Antarctic Continent, must belong to the entire continent the existence of which he revealed. Some geographers have recognized that part of Antarctica he discovered needed a special name and therefore gave it the name of Wilkes Land. When it is remembered that Wilkes changed the conception that the Antarctic was an ocean by demonstrating that it was a continent, the least that his discoveries demand is that the name of Wilkes Land be retained on all of Antarctica lying between the longitudes of 95° and 158° east.

THE GREAT ICE BARRIER

By Henry Gannett

IN his notable expedition of 1840 to the Antarctic, James Ross discovered a great ice cliff rising from the sea to an average height of nearly 200 feet and stretching from King Edward VII Land to South Victoria Land, a distance of about 400 nautical miles. Of its origin nothing was known, and, although later expeditions also visited it, they added little to our knowledge. It was not until Scott, in 1902, and Shackleton, in 1907, made their remarkable sledge journeys in the interior of Antarctica that the nature of the Great Ice Barrier became known.

The barrier is simply the southern limit of a great sheet of ice extending southward up a great bay which penetrates the land at least 300 miles and possibly double that distance. Indeed, it is possible that it may extend entirely across, joining with Weddell Sea on the opposite side and dividing Antarctica into two continents. From the barrier southward this bay, with a known area of at least 100,000 square miles, is entirely occupied by this ice sheet. It is bor-

dered on the west by high mountains from which stretches westward a still higher plateau, which reaches an altitude of over 11,000 feet at Shackleton's farthest southern point. The land on the east side of the bay is unknown, except at the point of King Edward VII Land, where the barrier joins it, but it also is probably mountainous.

From the high land on the west side numerous glaciers descend to this field of ice. Notable among them is that by which Shackleton ascended to the summit of the plateau in his wonderful sledge journey toward the South Pole, a glacier 100 miles long and 50 miles wide, with a descent of 8,000 feet. From the east side of the bay, and especially from its south end, probably other great glaciers contribute to the great ice field.

The name "Great Ice Barrier," originally applied only to the ice cliff forming its northern limit, has been extended and applied to the ice field itself, and even to the bay which it covers. It is unnecessary to say that these extensions in the application of the name are inap-

FRONT OF THE GREAT ICE BARRIER

propriate, and it is to be hoped that suitable names will be selected for these features. I would suggest for the ice field the name of Shackleton glacier, since Shackleton has made the most extensive explorations of it and its surroundings; moreover, I hope to show that it is in truth a glacier, although both Scott and Shackleton refuse to accept that explanation of the phenomenon. It is their belief that it has been formed from snow falling upon its surface much as the sea-ice of the Arctic is formed. But sea-ice nowhere accumulates to any such thickness as this or presents an ice wall at its borders. On the other hand, every glacier that reaches the sea presents just such an ice wall. There are scores of such glaciers on the Alaskan coast, and probably hundreds on Greenland, Grant Land, and Spitzbergen, whose fronts extend out into the sea, even into water so deep that they must be afloat, as is much of the barrier.

The snow which falls upon the surface of this ice field could not possibly supply the waste from the barrier, and another source of supply must be found. This supply is in the numerous and large stream glaciers which bring down the ice from the highlands on the east, west, and south of the bay. The area thus drained must be enormous—amply sufficient to maintain the supply.

The fact that this great ice field is moving northward at the rate of about one-third of a mile a year, as ascertained by Shackleton, would seem in itself as a conclusive demonstration that it is a glacier. Sea-ice, unless driven by wind or currents, is quiescent, while the glacier always moves toward lower levels.

Thus Shackleton glacier is a great mother glacier, into which drains the snow and ice from enormous areas of highland. This glacier collects the ice and transports it northward to the Great Ice Barrier, where it is dropped as bergs into Ross Sea.

THE RACE FOR THE SOUTH POLE

INTEREST in the American expedition to the South Polar regions has been very much increased during the past month by the coming to the United States of Sir Ernest H. Shackleton. This distinguished explorer gave his first lecture in America in Washington, March 26, to 5,000 members and guests of the National Geographic Society. At the conclusion of the address the President of the United States, on behalf of the Society, presented him with the Hubbard Gold Medal of the National Geographic Society, recently awarded Sir Ernest for his important discoveries in the Antarctic regions and for gaining farthest south—88° 23′—January 9, 1909.

"No private citizen has ever received a more auspicious welcome to America. Statesmen, diplomats, scientists, artists, men of letters, and men of distinction in every walk of life united in a great chorus of greeting to one of the most distinguished Englishmen of the present day. The audience included the President of the United States, Commander Robert E. Peary, the Ambassador of Great Britain and the entire staff of the British Embassy, the ambassadors of France, Germany, Japan, and Mexico, the ministers of Costa Rica, Portugal, Norway, The Netherlands, Denmark, Switzerland, and Sweden, the Secretary of the Treasury, the Secretary of War, the Secretary of the Navy, the Secretary of Commerce and Labor, the Admiral of the Navy, and many Members of Congress. Shackleton bore the honors crowded upon him with the spirit which he has shown since he emerged from the Antarctic regions nearly a year ago—with modesty and simple grace."

The expedition which formed the subject of his address has been fully described in previous numbers of the NATIONAL GEOGRAPHIC MAGAZINE.* Sir Ernest will repeat his lecture in many parts of the United States during April, May, and June.

His narrative is one of the most inspiring stories of adventure and accomplishment ever told, the courage, wit, pluck, resourcefulness, and good comradeship of the leader and his men making a most thrilling tale. Particularly interesting are moving pictures of the strange penguin, a bird 4 feet in height and weighing 90

*NAT. GEOG. MAG., April and November, 1909.

pounds, which cannot fly and waddles something like a seal.

Lieutenant Shackleton holds the record, not only for getting 400 miles nearer the South Pole than any of his predecessors, but also for the unparalleled importance of his contributions to scientific knowledge of conditions in the far south. The cost of his expedition was much greater than the funds he had personally raised, so that when he returned to England in 1909 he found himself $175,000 in debt. The British government knighted him for his achievements and made him a grant of $100,000. The balance he is now paying off by lectures and by his book, "The Heart of the Antarctic."

PRESENTATION OF THE
HUBBARD MEDAL BY PRESIDENT TAFT

Sir Ernest Shackleton: It is my pleasant duty to represent the National Geographic Society in presenting to you the evidence of its high appreciation of the marvelous work that you have done in the cause of science; and the endurance, courage, and intelligence shown in the pursuit of a definite object. I am sure that you will the more appreciate this medal, as it comes from the National Geographic Society, that has among its prominent members that distinguished American, Commander Robert E. Peary, who, while you were working at the South Pole, was himself surrounding the North Pole.

I do not know that nature had in mind the variety that was to be added to the lectures by the differences between her at the North Pole and at the South Pole, but certainly the different character of the surroundings of the North Pole and the South Pole make of entrancing interest the stories with respect to both.

You will permit me, therefore, to have the honor of handing you the medal of the Society, which gives its evidence of how highly they appreciate your services to science and to mankind.

RESPONSE BY SIR ERNEST SHACKLETON.

Mr. President: It is a very great honor for me to have this medal from the National Geographic Society, and especially as it is given to me by the hands of the distinguished President of the United States. It could not mean more for me than to have it given in this way in this great hall. But while I am standing I would like to say that Commander Peary will have as warm a welcome over in England as I have received from your great American society tonight. Commander Peary's work belongs not only to America, but to the world.

We are all pleased, and we wish, of course, a good measure of success to any forthcoming American expedition to the South Polar regions, because they have got a very hard job to tackle on the other side.

And, sir, I thank you. It is a very great honor to me. I thank you very much for having presented this medal.

THE RACE FOR THE SOUTH POLE

During the past month each member of the National Geographic Society has received an invitation to subscribe to the American expedition to the South Pole under the auspices of the Peary Arctic Club and the National Geographic Society. Such generous responses have been received from a large body of the memhers that it is believed the expedition will be able to leave in September.

Sufficient funds at this writing have, however, not been secured, and those members of the Society who are interested in the work and have not yet sent in their subscriptions are earnestly requested to do so immediately. The subscriptions range from $1.00 to $500. While large subscriptions are welcome, the Society hopes that all members will be sufficiently interested to subscribe from $1.00 to $5.00.

The reasons why an expedition should leave this year are as follows:

1. The expedition can be equipped at approximately one-half the cost necessary to equip an expedition any other year, owing to the fact that the *Roosevelt* and all the material used on Commander Peary's last expedition are immediately available.

2. Peary's four lieutenants—Captain Bartlett, George Borup, McMillan, and Doctor Goodsell—and practically the entire crew of the last expedition are eager to join the American South Polar Expedition, provided it can leave this year. The American party could thus take advantage of men whose experience in polar work is unequalled.

3. From a scientific point of view, tidal and magnetic observations obtained at the same time that the English expedition are making simultaneous records on the other side of the South Pole will be vastly more important than if taken during another year, when there is no other expedition in the south. Similarly the work of the British expedition will be benefited by the American.

4. As Sir Ernest Shackleton has said, every step taken by the American expedition from its proposed base on the shores of Weddell Sea will be an entirely new discovery. No region in the world offers such an opportunity for the acquiring of new knowledge.

SOUTH POLAR EXPLORATIONS

THREE expeditions, a British, a Japanese, and a Norwegian, will be struggling during the next 12 months to reach the South Pole. Unfortunately for scientific purposes, all three are endeavoring to gain the goal by practically the same route—from the vicinity of Mount Erebus over the great ice barrier, and then up over the great inland plateau. This is the route discovered by Scott and Shackleton, and over which the latter gained a point within 97 miles of the Pole in 1909.

The British expedition is led by Capt. Robert F. Scott, of the Royal Navy, who directed the very successful British party of 1901–'04.

SEAL SUCKLING YOUNG AND TAKING NO NOTICE OF THE MOTOR CAR

SEALS EMERGING FROM THE WATER AT THEIR BLOW-HOLES, NEAR MOUNT EREBUS

Two years were spent in preparations for this last expedition, which left England in June, 1910. The party comprises 60 persons, including a large number of scientists and scientific assistants. They are provisioned for three years, and are using as their headquarters the same base that was occupied by Scott, 1901–'04, and by Shackleton, 1908–'09.

The *Terra Nova*, which has recently returned after landing Scott's sledge parties, reports that Amundsen, the leader of the Norwegian party, is also camped near by. Amundsen, it will be remembered, had been planning for several years to reach the North Pole by drifting across it. When he left Europe on the *Fram* in 1910, it was with the announced intention of proceeding around Cape Horn, thence up the Pacific through Bering Strait into the Arctic Ocean, where he was to allow his ship to be frozen in the ice. He was provisioned for five years, at the end of which time he expected to have drifted across the North Polar area and to be freed in the vicinity of Iceland or Norway. But from Madeira Amundsen cabled that he had altered his plans and would spend a year endeavoring to reach the South Pole. It is presumed that he sought to land his party on King Ed-

ward VII Land, some distance from Scott's intended headquarters, but, like all explorers who have preceded him in this region, failed to find a satisfactory point for disembarking, and was compelled to continue along the great ice barrier to Mount Erebus.

The cabled advices have stated that Amundsen was to inaugurate his attack upon the Pole immediately, not waiting for the winter to pass before beginning his advance. From this we infer that he intends to take advantage of moonlight and advance depots of supplies up the route during the brighter periods of the polar night. Previous South Polar expeditions have confined their explorations almost entirely to daylight, though Peary's success in gaining high latitudes in the Arctics was largely due to the fact that he kept his sledging parties at work dtiriug the full moon.

The Japanese party is led by Lieutenant Shirase. Like Amundsen's, it is small in numbers. Shirase has not had the training in icework that Scott and Amundsen have experienced, and it is doubtful whether the heroic spirit of his party can prevail against the lack of equipment.

AMUNDSEN'S ATTAINMENT
OF THE SOUTH POLE

THIS page was already on the press when the cable came from New Zealand announcing the attainment of the South Pole by Roald Amundsen, December 14–17, 1911. Amundsen is a gold medalist of the National Geographic Society, having been awarded the Hubbard Medal of the Society for his achievement of the Northwest Passage from the Atlantic to the Pacific, and for his explorations and observations on that remarkable voyage of discovery. The Society rejoices at his well-earned success in attaining the coveted goal at the far South.

Many geographers had feared that Amundsen would yield to the temptation of following, for a considerable part of the way to the South Pole, the route previously discovered and opened by Shackleton; but his account shows that he was not satisfied to do this, and in consequence he has made discoveries and surveys that are entirely new.

The whole distance traversed by him—approximately 700 miles from his base, where he moored his ship to ice-front—to the pole itself, appears to have been across previously untraversed and unknown ice and land. He has defined the eastern and southern boundaries of the Great Ice Barrier, that vast plain of floating ice which flows down from the great Antarctic Continent, and whose western boundary had been defined previously by Shackleton. This enormous glacial ice plain is one of the wonders of the world. It is a solid mass of ice, floating for the most part, approximately 800 to 1,600 feet thick, and covering an area of about 100,000 square miles, or considerably larger than New York, Massachusetts, New Hampshire, and Vermont combined.

Amundsen found traveling across the barrier comparatively easy. He marched 382 geographical miles due south across the plain until he was confronted by the high mountains. Here he was so fortunate as to find a glacier route up to the inland plateau easier than the Beardmore Glacier, which was used by Shackleton to ascend to the inland plateau three years before.

Amundsen and four companions accomplished the ascent from the ice plain to the pla-

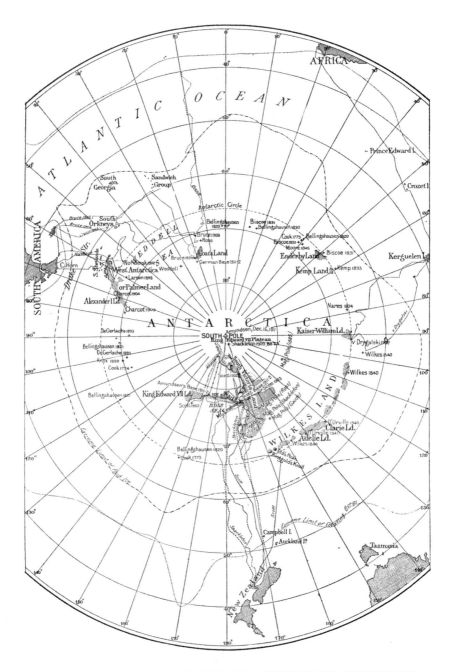

OUTLINE MAP SHOWING ROUTE OF AMUNDSEN TO SOUTH POLE

Captain Scott's base is also shown. Scott was planning to follow the route of Shackleton. The Japanese South Polar expedition is now campcd near Amundsen's base; the Australian expedition has made a base on Clarie Land; the base of the German expedition is on the other side of the continent on Coats Land.

92

teau, 10,500 feet, in the marvelously short time of four days. He was now about 275 miles from the pole, and thence onward his greatest difficulties were encountered. The rare atmosphere at this high elevation made breathing difficult. Storms delayed them, but they pushed on and reached the pole December 14, staying there for three days. The pole is at an elevation of 10,500 feet. Amundsen reports a lofty chain of mountains, some attaining 15,000 feet, extending southeastward as far as he could see. The chain is probably an extension of the lofty range seen by Shackleton, and probably stretches across the South Polar area to Waddell Sea.

Shackleton in 1909 reached a point so near the South Pole that we have known pretty accurately the conditions at that extreme point, so that the part of Amundsen's narrative dealing with the pole itself, while highly entertaining, is not so important or so novel as it would otherwise have been.

Amundsen owes his success to his very carefully prepared equipment, to his splendid dogs and his skill in handling them, and to many years of previous experience in battling with the ice and snow of the far North. Next to Peary, he is the most experienced traveler on ice in the world. The following notes from his cable to the New York *Times*, to whom the world is indebted for his story, illustrate the minute care with which every detail was anticipated:

"Washing was a luxury never indulged in on the journey, nor was there any shaving; but, as the beard has to be kept short, to prevent ice accumulating from one's breath, a beard-cutting machine which we had taken along proved invaluable. Another article taken was a tooth extractor, and this also proved valuable, for one man had a tooth which became so bad that it was absolutely essential that it should be pulled out, and this could hardly have been done without a proper instrument.

"For food we relied entirely on pemmican, biscuits, chocolate, powdered milk, and, of course, dog meat. The dogs were fed on pemmican.

"In my opinion we had the best and most satisfying provisions possible. In fact, from the beginning to the end of the journey we never felt an undue craving for something to eat or any feeling of not having had sufficient nourishment."

AMERICAN DISCOVERERS
OF THE ANTARCTIC CONTINENT

By Major General A. W. Greely, U. S. Army

"When I refuse, for any cause, the homage due to American talent, or abate the tithe of a hair from just character or just fame, may my tongue cleave to the roof of my mouth."

—Webster.

CLOSE on the news of the American discovery of the North Pole by Robert E. Peary comes by cable from Australia the intensely interesting story of the conquest of the South Pole by that chief of the Norse vikings of today—Captain Roald Amundsen. Entering the broad field of Antarctic research, with keen perception and sound judgment he has profited by the experiences of his British predecessors, introducing innovations as to equipment methods, field work, and lines of approach.

His wisely chosen route to the Pole was due to a sagacious recognition of the fact that the great oceanic ice-cap known as Ross' barrier, flowing from the southeast, is diverted from its course by the mountainous coast of South Victoria Land, whose outlying cliffs are ground by the almost irresistible force of the barrier.

The onward movement of this inconceivably enormous body of solid ice, estimated by some to have a superficial area of 100,000 square miles, naturally produces fathomless fissures in and great upheavals on the surface of the barrier bordering Victoria Land, while the eastern sections along the coast of King Edward VII Land remain in a state of comparative quiescence, with its surface unbroken by pressure and unmarked by crevasses.

Again should be noted Amundsen's originality in locating his winter home on the ice-barrier and his restless energy during the autumn in establishing advance depots on the colorless, unmarked ice-plain, with signals insuring their attainment after their burial by the winter snows.

While displaying high qualities of resourcefulness and unusual powers of endurance, Amundsen's human attributes are most admirable and have won universal esteem and applause. One reads with pleasure the plain, straightforward story of his onward march and final success, told with unfeigned modesty, and further notes with intense satisfaction the absence of any assertive superiority over his friendly rivals, whose fortunes he views with a manly and generous spirit.

And so the whole world unites in homage of the highest character to this Norwegian sailor for his contributions to knowledge—contributions gained by such personal sacrifices of physical, financial, and self-denying character.

Another page of Antarctic history—which, though supplementary to the attainment of the pole, is of absorbing interest, especially to Americans—was written a week after Amundsen's return. A cablegram from Hobart, Tasmania, dated March 12, 1912, ran as follows: "The Australian expedition ship *Aurora*, concerning which there had been some anxiety, returned to Hobart today, after landing Dr. Douglas Mawson, the leader of the expedition and of the party, January 19, on Adélie Land, and another party under Dr. White (Wild?), February 19, on Termination Land, discovered by the American Captain Wilkes, in 1840, on the edge of the glacier."

Among Antarctic explorers, Amundsen and Mawson would be the last to fail in homage to and in just appreciation of the invaluable work done during the past century by their predecessors. That work made possible the magnificent successes of Amundsen in reaching the physical Pole in 1911, and of Mawson's attainment

of the South Magnetic Pole, in 1909, in 72° 25′ S. latitude, 155° 16′ E. longitude, and also his later scientific expedition to Wilkes' Southern Continent.

ENLIGHTENMENT ESSENTIAL TO NATIONAL HONOR

History reveals many instances in which not only individuals but also nations have failed to receive, or been temporarily deprived of, honor due for important additions to human knowledge or advances in the march of civilization.

When recorded history began, there were four continents unknown whose subsequent discoveries have been of unsurpassing geographic importance. As regards the two Americas, the rightful honor pertains to Spain, as is universally known. In the case of Australia, priority is unknown, claims being made by France, Holland, Portugal, and Spain.

With reference to Antarctica, through misinformation and neglect in the past, our countrymen have failed to pay "the homage due to American talent." The object of this brief memoir is to clearly and concisely present such facts as may conserve to America the rightful honor of both the original discovery of Antarctica as well as of first ascertaining and making known its definite existence as a continent.

Australian energy and courage, by the recent occupation of Termination Land for scientific research, have thus put an end to the anti-American campaign of many years' duration. During this period American honor has suffered from national neglect as well as from unwarranted assertions and disingenuous representations from foreign sources, thus beclouding the situation to American discredit. Moreover, claims have been made which attribute to European activities that priority of Antarctic discoveries which rightfully pertains to American explorers.

PALMER'S DISCOVERY
OF THE ANTARCTIC CONTINENT IN 1821

The earliest phase of American Antarctic exploration was due to the ambitious energies of Connecticut whalers, whose commercial and professional instincts impelled them to seek an extension of profitable sealing grounds. As is well known, the daring pioneer voyages of American fishermen successfully exploited in the 19th century even the most remote seas, and thus brought into our national coffers whaling products to the value of 332 millions of dollars from 1804 to 1876.

The discovery of the sealing grounds of the South Shetlands (see map, page 92) promptly attracted a fleet of New England whalers, which established its base of operations at Deception Island, where seals were so plentiful that 50,598 sealskins were taken in one season, 1820–1821. The smallest vessel of the fleet was the sloop *Hero*, 44.5 tons, commanded by a youth of 21 years, Capt. Nathaniel Brown Palmer. While at the lookout maintained on the volcanic crater near Yankee Harbor, one of the sealing captains, Benjamin Pendleton, on a clear day discovered snow-capped peaks outlined against the southern horizon.

Realizing that the wholesale destruction of seals must soon exhaust the local supply, Captain Palmer, in an interval of fine weather, sailed southward, in January, 1821, to search for new fishing grounds. Reaching the new and hitherto unknown land, only some 70 miles distant, Palmer skirted its northwestern coasts, which he found to be a mountainous, snow-covered region, entered several bays, and saw sea leopards, though finding no seals. His far-

thest point in that voyage was about 68° S. latitude, 59° W. longitude. In his homeward passage Palmer fell in with the Russian exploring expedition commanded by Capt. F. G. von Bellingshausen, which, after an unparalleled voyage through Antarctic waters, had discovered the islands of Peter I and of Alexander. These were possibly the first seen, and certainly the first charted and named, land within the Antarctic circle. Palmer gave Bellingshausen full information as to his own voyage and discoveries.

Dr. Hugh Robert Mill, in his generally accurate and fair-minded "Siege of the South Pole," 1905, unfortunately follows the British attitude of indirectly discrediting Palmer's story as to the Russian admiral, saying (page 100): "It seems strange that if informed of the whereabouts of Palmer Land he (Bellingshausen) made no reference to that fact in his own book."

However, Dr. Henryk Arctowski, a Belgian professor, a Russian scholar, and an Antarctic explorer and expert, supports Palmer by a citation. In "The Antarctic Voyage of the *Belgica*" (in the *Geographical Journal*, 1901, 18:353–394), Arctowski states that "this meeting was also described by Bellingshausen himself, as can easily be seen by consulting the remarkable but still little-known work of that eminent Russian explorer (Dwukratnyja, 2:262–264)." It is to be regretted that Dr. Mill failed to verify the citation.

Mr. E. S. Balch, in his scholarly study ("Antarctica," Phila., 1902, page 95), admirably summarizes the results of Palmer's voyages. He ascribes to him, with undoubted accuracy:

1. Certainly the first explorer of the land lying south of Bransfield Strait, and extending for some 250 kilometers (over 150 miles) between about 57° 50′ and 62° 20′ west longi-

tude; that is, of the northern coasts of West Antarctica from Liege Island to Joinville Island, both inclusive.

2. Discovered the northern end of Gerlache Strait.

3. Discovered the strait since called Orléans Channel. He also accurately adds: "This coast or these islands were christened Palmer Land, and they were so first charted in England, France, and America."

Palmer never realized that he had discovered a continent, and had thus placed his name among the immortals. Even after the discoveries of Wilkes, he claimed, in 1847, only the discovery of Palmer Land and the credit of sailing into the Antarctic Ocean to the distance of 340 miles southwest from Yankee Harbor.

However, Captains Edmund Fanning and Benjamin Morrell, contemporaneous whalers with Palmer, considered the land continental. The former writer says (Fanning: "Voyages," page 476): "From information that the author has in his possession it is presumed that the continent of Palmer Land does not extend further west than the 100th degree of west longitude." He adds: "It is reported that an extensive bank, with from 60 to 100 fathoms of water over it, has been discovered between the latitude of 66° and 69° south, to the westward of 140° west longitude, which may be connected with extensive land to the south of it."[1]

---

1. Attempts have been made to discredit Fanning, a sealer, making no claims to scientific accuracy in astronomical positions. His general statements are strikingly confirmed by the discovery by the *Belgica*, under Gerlache, of a continental plateau, from 75° to 103° W. (the *Belgica*'s farthest), sloping gently to the south, with soundings from 100 to 250 fathoms. Unquestionably the plateau extends farther west.

Long designated as insular, the continental character of Palmer Land has been gradually proved through the discoveries of Larsen, 1893; of Nordenskiöld, 1903, and of Charcot, 1910.

As it is now acknowledged that this land is a northerly projection of the continent of Antarctica, to this American sea captain must be given geographic credit second to the other only known discoverer of a continent—Christopher Columbus—who no more than Palmer realized the greatness of his work.

HOW PALMER LAND
BECAME GRAHAM LAND

Among the curious recurrence of parallels in history is the surprising fact that the only men who have discovered continents—Columbus, the unknown discoverer of Australia, and Palmer—should each have failed in receiving that highest form of geographical homage—the application of their names to the lands discovered.

A fellow-explorer, the English sailor George Powell, fittingly honored his American comrade by charting "Palmer Land" on his map of South Shetlands, 1822, which nomenclature was promptly accepted in French official publications ("Annales Maritimes et Coloniales," Paris, 1824).

The just and accurate use of Palmer Land continued on the charts of the world until, in 1831, it was displaced by potent authorities. The Enderby brothers, of Great Britain, one of whom was an influential Fellow of the Royal Geographical Society, fitted out an expedition under command of John Biscoe, a retired master of the Royal Navy, who visited the coasts of Palmer Land, whence resulted its replacement by Graham Land, renamed after the

TWO EMPEROR PENGUINS ON SOUTH VICTORIA LAND

first Lord of the Admiralty, Sir James R. G. Graham.

The combination of the British government, of the Royal Navy, and of the Royal Geographical Society was overpowering, so that the name of the American captain disappeared from Antarctic charts, of which England then had a practical monopoly. The potency of the authority of the "mistress of the seas" and the insidious effect of this act of suppression and unjustifiable substitution can be traced through the geographic literature of the past 8o years. The *Encyclopedia Britannica*, 9th edition, 1875, mentions neither Palmer nor charts his discoveries.

Nor has the influence of such suppression been confined to Europe, as its effect has been often noted in this country. In March, 1912, one of the best-edited and most reliable of American newspapers published a long and detailed summary of Antarctic explorations, widely copied, in which neither the name nor the work of the discoverer of Antarctica is even mentioned. On the contrary, to the Russian explorer Bellingshausen is indirectly ascribed the honor which pertains to an American sailor.

One English author, Dr. Hugh Robert Mill ("Siege of the South Pole," 1905, page 162), expresses the opinion that as a matter of historic justice it seems to us that Powell's name of Palmer Land ought to be retained," an opinion inseparable from any careful consideration of the facts.

The standard British authority for south-polar work is *The Antarctic Manual*, specially compiled for the governmental expedition of 1901, commanded by Captain R. F. Scott, R. N. It reproduces on its charts the tracks and discoveries of all the British whalers, including Biscoe, who appropriated Palmer's work. It omits from the charts Palmer's name, although

the contribution of the Belgian professor, Arctowski, to the manual mentions Palmer Land in text and by sketch map.

A concession is made in the *Encyclopedia Britannica*, 11th edition, 1911, specially Americanized for the United States, which admits in two lines that "Nathaniel Brown Palmer discovered the mountainous *archipelago* which now bears his name." It then proceeds to give a column regarding John Biscoe, R. N., whose explorations, as above recited, displaced Palmer Land in favor of Graham *Land*.

Has not the time arrived when the glorious phase of American maritime history should receive full national recognition? Every textbook teaching polar geography should contain the statement that the American captain, N. B. Palmer, first discovered parts of the continent of Antarctica, and on every official south-polar map should be replaced Palmer Land.

ANTARCTIC DISCOVERIES BY LIEUTENANT CHARLES WILKES, U. S. NAVY

We pass now to the American who discovered widely separated points of Antarctica. Realizing with scientific acumen their interrelations, he correctly designated the new regions as the Antarctic Continent.

The Wilkes expedition for maritime exploration was authorized by an act of Congress approved May 18, 1836. As organized, it consisted of five unsuitable and inadequately equipped ships, of which the largest was the flagship *Vincennes* and the smallest the *Flying Fish*, 96 tons. The command was refused by several officers, but late in 1838 the squadron sailed under Lieut. Charles Wilkes, U. S. Navy. Scientific work was strictly subordinated to surveys and explorations, it being a commercial enterprise.

The official instructions of the Secretary of Navy, Paulding, August 11, 1838, ran in part as follows:

"You will proceed to explore the southern Antarctic to the southward of Powell's group, and between it and Sandwich Land, endeavoring to reach a high southern latitude, making such examination and surveys of the bays, ports, inlets, and sounds in that region (Tierra del Fuego) as may be serviceable in future to vessels engaged in the whale fisheries.

"From Sydney (at the end of 1839) you will make a second attempt to penetrate within the Antarctic region, south of Van Dieman's Land, and as far west as longitude 45° E., or to Enderby Land. The Congress of the United States, having in view the important interests of our commerce embarked in the whale fisheries and other adventures in the great Southern Ocean, by an act of the 18th of May, 1836, authorized an expedition to be fitted out for the purpose of exploring and surveying that sea.

"Although the primary object of the expedition is the promotion of the great interests of commerce and navigation, yet you will take all occasions not incompatible with the great purposes of your undertaking to extend the bounds

EMPERORS ON THE MARCH

DIGGING TO ASCERTAIN THE DEPTH OF SNOW
COVERING A DEPOT LEFT BY A PREVIOUS EXPEDITION

of science and promote the acquisition of knowledge.

"You will prohibit all under your command from furnishing any person not belonging to the expedition with information which has reference to the objects or proceedings of the expedition."

While no mention was made of Palmer's discoveries, they were well known to Wilkes, who made Orange Harbor, Tierra del Fuego, his base of operations. With the *Porpoise* and *Sea Gull* he explored to the east. Leaving South Shetlands to the north on March 3, 1839, Wilkes reports: "Filled away at daylight, and stood for Palmer Land. . . . At 6:30 we made land, which I took to be Mount Hope, the eastern point of Palmer Land. . . . Near to us we discovered three small islets, and gave them the name of Adventure Islets, while beyond and above all rose two high mountains, one of which was Mt. Hope."

Violent gales and thick ice obliged a speedy return.

Meanwhile Captain Hudson, in the *Peacock*, and Lieutenant Walker, in the *Flying Fish*, struggled southwestward from February 25 to March 25, with gales and fogs. Appearances of land (unconfirmed) were noted from about 70° 20′ S., 100° W.

The next Antarctic cruise was made from Sydney, Australia, the designated base. Wilkes sailed December 26, 1839, with the flagship *Vincennes*, the *Peacock*, the *Porpoise*, and the tiny pilot-boat *Flying Fish*.

This memoir does not concern the dangers and privations incident to this astonishing Antarctic cruise, from which one ship returned almost as by miracle. Nevertheless, unfitness of ships, insufficiency of clothing, inappropriate food, inclemency of weather, extraordinary ice conditions, and difficulties of navigating sailing ships in the ice form a background against which stand out brilliantly the indomitable character of the commander, the courage, seamanship, and resourcefulness of the officers and men. Attention is here given only to discoveries.

This account is drawn from Wilkes' narrative, and quotations are from the reports of proceedings by the ships named.

January 16, 1840. "Appearances believed to be land were visible from all three vessels."[2]

January 19, 1840. "In the morning we (*Vincennes*) found ourselves in a deep bay. Land was now certainly visible, both to the south-southeast and southwest, in the former direction most distinctly. Both appeared high."

At three the same morning Hudson, in the *Peacock*, tacked to reach "An immense mass which had every appearance of land, seen far beyond and towering over an ice island. It bore southwest and had the appearance of being 3,000 feet in height, looking gray and dark, and divided into two distinct ridges throughout its entire extent; the whole being covered with snow."[3]

January 22, 1840. "The *Peacock* stood into the (Peacock) bay and saw the same appearance of high land in the distance. Sounded; bottom was reached at 320 fathoms; the matter brought up was slate-covered mud." (The bay, 20 miles deep, was surrounded by an ice-barrier.)

2. The *Flying Fish* was absent. The land signs are surmised to have been the loom of the Balleny Islands, discovered the previous January, but unknown to Wilkes.

3. Admiral John E. Pillsbury, U. S. Navy, conclusively proves (NATIONAL GEOGRAPHIC MAGAZINE, February, 1910, pp. 171–173) from D'Urville's reports that his discovery of Adélie Land was one day after Wilkes discovered Cape Hudson. D'Urville used the date of America, and Wilkes that of Europe, so that D'Urville's January 21 was in reality January 22.

January 23, 1840. The *Vincennes* entered an indentation in the ice-barrier, which stretched unbroken along their course.

"The appearance of land was observed both to the eastward and westward. . . . Reached the solid barrier. This was a deep indentation in the coast, about 25 miles wide; explored it to the depth of 15 miles. This I have called Disappointment Bay; it is in latitude 67° 4′ 3″ S., longitude 147° 30′ E."

January 28, 1840. The *Vincennes* at 9:30 a. m. "had another sight of land ahead. (11 a. m.) We had the land now in plain view." A violent gale obliged the ship to put to sea.

January 30, 1840. From the *Vincennes* "land was in sight. At 8 o'clock reached the icy barrier and hove to. It was tantalizing, with the land in sight, to be again and again blocked out. . . . This bay was formed partly by rocks and partly by ice islands. . . . We approached within half a mile of the dark volcanic rocks, which appeared on both sides of us, and saw the land gradually rising beyond the ice to the height of 3,000 feet, and entirely covered with snow. . . . I make this bay (called Piner) in longitude 140° 2′ 30″ E., latitude 66° 45′ S.; and now that all are convinced of its existence, *I gave the land the name of the Antarctic Continent.* . . . Sounded and found a hard bottom at 30 fathoms."

Driven from Piner Bay by a gale, Wilkes continued his cruise along the unbroken ice-barrier to the westward. This, in despite of the official report of his medical officers, endorsed by a majority of his line officers, that "a few days more of such exposure . . . would reduce the number of the crew by sickness to such an extent as to hazard the safety of the ship and the lives of all on board."

February 2, 1840. The *Vincennes* in 137° 2′ E., 66° 12′ S., at 3 p. m., had "land in sight, with the same lofty appearance as before. No break in the icy barrier, where a foot could be set on the rocks."

February 6, 1840. From the *Vincennes* the barrier "still had the appearance of being attached to the land, and in one uninterrupted line."

February 7, 1840. The *Vincennes* "continued all day running along the perpendicular icy barrier, about 150 feet in height. Beyond it the outline of the high land could be well distinguished. At 6 p. m. we found the barrier suddenly trending to the southward. . . . This point I have named Cape Carr, in longitude 131° 40′ E., latitude 64° 49′ S."

February 8, 1840. The *Vincennes* at noon was in 127° 7′ E., 65° 3′ S. "At 7 p. m. we had strong indications of land; the barrier was of the former perpendicular form, and later the outline of the continent appeared distinct though distant."

February 12, 1840. From the *Vincennes* at 1 p. m.: "Land was now distinctly seen from 18 to 20 miles distant, bearing from south-southeast to southwest—a lofty mountain range, covered with snow, though showing many ridges and indentations. . . . The barrier in places had the appearance of being broken up, and we had decreased our longitude to 112° 16′ 12″ E., while our latitude was 64° 57′ S. This put the land in about 65° 20′ S., and its trending nearly east and west."

February 13, 1840. The *Vincennes* "in the afternoon had the land ahead. At 6.30 p. m. it was judged to be 10 or 12 miles distant. The day was remarkably clear and the land very distinct. By measurement we made the extent of coast of the Antarctic Continent, which was then in sight, 75 miles, and by approximate measurement 3,000 feet high. It was entirely covered with snow.

A RACING TEAM: CAPE NOME, ALASKA

Amundsen, on his journey to the South Pole, averaged 15½ miles per march. On his return he averaged 22 miles, on one march making 31 miles. No previous explorer in the south has made distances like these. Peary's average on his return from the North Pole to land was 25.6 miles. On one of his earlier expeditions Peary made the distance from Cape Wilkes to Cape D'Urville, a distance of 65 miles, in one march. He repeatedly made distances of 40 miles in one march, and in the winter of 1899–1900 traveled from Etah to a point in Robertson Bay, 60 miles distant, in less than 12 hours. On the Greenland ice-cap he once averaged 20 miles a day for 25 successive marches, and on another occasion he averaged 30 miles a day in seven successive marches. Macmillan and Borup, members of the last Peary expedition, returning from Cape Morris Jessup to the *Roosevelt*, made the distance of 250 miles in eight marches, an average of over 31 miles a march.

Longitude at noon, 106° 18′ 42″ E., latitude 65° 49′ 40″ S. . . . Hove to. Fortunately made a landing (on an ice island). We found imbedded in it boulders, stones, etc. There was no doubt that it had been detached from the land, which was about 8 miles distant."

Wilkes turned back when in about 97° 40′ E. longitude, 64° 1′ S. latitude, having traced for 1,700 miles a practically uninterrupted ice-barrier, bordering the coast of his Antarctic Continent.

The *Vincennes* proceeded first to Hobart Town, then to Sydney, which it reached on March 11. Lieutenant Wilkes immediately announced the discovery of a South Polar Continent to the Secretary of the Navy in the following letter, dated at Sydney, New South Wales, March 11, 1840:

"It affords me much gratification to report that *we have discovered a large body of land within the Antarctic circle, which I have named the Antarctic Continent*, and refer you to the report of our cruise and accompanying charts, inclosed herewith, for full information relative thereto."

Mr. Edwin S. Balch, in his learned and exhaustive memoir on south-polar explorations (*Antarctica*, Phila., 1902) most concisely and justly summarized the geographical outcome of this cruise in the statement: "The cruise of Wilkes will remain among the remarkable voyages of all time. No finer achievement has been accomplished in the annals of the Arctic or of the Antarctic. With unsuitable, improperly equipped ships, amid icebergs, gales, snowstorms, and fogs, Wilkes followed an unknown coast-line for a distance exceeding in length the Ural Mountain range. It is the long distance which Wilkes traversed which makes the results of his cruise so important; for he did not merely sight the coast in one or two places, but he hugged it for such a distance as to make sure that the land was continental in dimensions. . . . It is only the exact truth to assert that the honor of recognizing the existence of the continent of Antarctica belongs to Charles Wilkes and to the United States Exploring Expedition."

DISCOVERIES OF WILKES DISCREDITED

On his announcement of the existence of the Antarctic Continent, Wilkes naturally expected an appreciative acknowledgment and high commendation—from his own countrymen at least. Instead his experiences were practically parallel with those of Columbus. Placed in arrest, he was tried for his commission under charges alleging cruelty, falsehood, grave misconduct, and of scandalous acts—such, for instance, as wearing the uniform of a captain while yet a lieutenant. After a long and exhaustive trial he was fully and honorably acquitted, though he suffered from the chagrin and temporary stigma incident to such official investi-

gations. Though reëstablished in public opinion at home, he was subject to attacks and innuendoes from abroad to the day of his death.

By extending an unexpected favor Wilkes gained an enemy. Contrary to his stringent official instructions, he sent to Capt. J. C. Ross, R. N., then engaged in Antarctic research, a chart and letter showing his own experiences and discoveries. This officer of the Royal Navy not only reflected severely on Wilkes (Ross: "Voyage to the South Seas," 1847, I:272, 280, 285–299), but omitted all of his discoveries from the admiralty chart, on which appeared those of every British sealer.

His brilliant successes in Arctic and in Antarctic explorations place Ross in a class by himself in polar annals. But unwisely he derogated from his glory by unjustly attributing to Wilkes a dishonorable intrusion on this field of work in 1840. As Wilkes was acting under official orders of 1836, this was clearly an unfounded aspersion which ultimately resulted in the condemnation of Ross' action by competent critics in England, France, and America.

Wilkes, in his "Synopsis of Cruise," 1842, clearly says that on the chart sent to Ross was "laid down land not only where we had determined it to exist, but those places in which every appearance denoted its existence," as was natural in a chart for information. Ross declined this explanation, and then unfortunately charted himself the Parry Mountains, which are nonexistent. (Scott: "Voyage of the Discovery," I:171).

Thus it was Ross, not Wilkes, who appropriated other men's discoveries, for three of Ross' new islands are only three peaks of Balleny's Sturge Island (Scott: "Voyage of the Discovery," II:389).

The discrediting of Wilkes by standard English authorities has been bold, open, and persistent for 70 years, though occasionally in late years some able, impartial expert, like the Scotch scientist, Sir John Murray, has expressed belief in him.

The *Encyclopedia Britannica*, 9th edition, 1875, says of Wilkes' discovery of the southern continent: "As a portion of it had already been seen by Balleny and the rest of it has since been proved not to exist, the claim has not been admitted." Balleny's mate, John McNab, however, when in 65° 10′ S., 117° 4′ E., on March 3, 1839, records in his journal, "To the southwest the ice was quite fast, with every *appearance* of land at the back of it, but the weather coming on thick." And on this indefinite statement British geographers locate Sabrina Land and declare it to be *known* land.

In 1897, in his anniversary address to the Royal Geographical Society, its president, Sir Clements Markham, claimed that Sir James Clark Ross, R. N., "made one of the greatest of geographical discoveries of modern times, amid regions of perpetual ice, *including a southern continent*."

In 1899 Markham read before the International Geographical Congress at Berlin a paper, "The Antarctic Expeditions," in which he omitted the names of Wilkes and Palmer. Moreover, he proposed to divide the Antarctic region into four quadrants, and to name each quadrant after an eminent Britisher. He eliminated Wilkes' discoveries and proposed to call the region which Wilkes had explored "Victoria Quadrant," thus ignoring the prior and brilliant work of the great Antarctic French explorer, Dumont D'Urville, as well as that of the American.

The Antarctic Manual, 1901, compiled for the British National Antarctic Expedition of that year, omits from its official chart all of Wilkes' discoveries except Knox Land.

The 30-inch British terrestrial globe, by W. and A. K. Johnson, corrected to 1903, omits all of Wilkes' work.

Capt. R. E Scott, R. N., in his "Voyage of the Discovery," 1905, states of his own cruise: "Thus once and for all we have definitely disposed of Wilkes Land," and so omits it from his chart, retaining Sabrina Land, however, of Balleny.[4]

With unconscious inconsistency Scott admits that "Wilkes' soundings still remain as a guide to the limit of the continental plateau," thus indirectly assuming that Ross discovered the austral continent.

Dr. Mill, "Siege of the South Pole," 1905, indefinitely admits that Wilkes discovered something, but does not directly name any land. Ignoring entirely the official chart of Wilkes, Mill gives a misleading impression by reproducing without explanation the preliminary chart sent to Ross (Balch: Antarctica, 1902). Sir Ernest Shackleton accepts Scott's erroneous statement about sailing "over part of the so-called Wilkes Land," "The Heart of the Antarctic," page 229, and omits it from his chart (except Knox Land), but sympathizingly adds, "The question of the existence of this land in any other position had been left open."

The first break in nearly fourscore years of misrepresentation in British standard works is in the *Encyclopedia Britannica*, 11th edition, 1911, where Dr. Mill admits "there can be no doubt that Wilkes saw land along the line where Adélie Land, Kemp Land, Enderby Land are known

---

4. Mr. Edwin Swift Balch, in his "Why America Should Re-explore Wilkes Land," p. 39, etc., shows that Scott never reached Wilkes Land.

KILLER WHALES SOUNDING OFF THE GREAT ICE BARRIER

to exist, even if the positions he assigns are not quite accurate."

THE CONTINENT OF ANTARCTICA

Probably no other standard authority denies the existence of a south-polar continent save the *Encyclopedia Britannica*, 11th edition, 1911, which mentions "Australia, the *only* continent entirely in the southern hemisphere." The 10th edition, 1902, said: "The hypothesis of a great Antarctic continent, or continental archipelago, continuously covered by an ice-sheet, is confirmed by the observations of recent explorers, but the evidence is not yet direct or conclusive."

Nearly 40 years since, a distinguished scientist, born on the continent of North America, Sir John Murray, of *Challenger* expedition and fame, and one of the eight honorary members of the National Geographic Society, considered the mooted extent of south polar lands and finally outlined their logical continental form as the continent of Antarctica—a fitting and largely accepted name. This great feat of constructive geography depended on a few-score handfuls of oceanic ooze from the south-polar seas and scanty bits of rocks from scattered lands.

Whatever doubts remained as to the accuracy of Murray's deductions have disappeared since the cumulative discoveries of Amundsen, Borchgrevink, Bruce, Drygalski, Gerlache, Larsen, Nordenskiöld, Scott, and Shackleton. Indeed, a German scientist has calculated that

Antarctica is considerably greater in area than Europe, and that the average elevation is more than double that of Asia.

CONCLUSION

It has been shown that the primary discovery of Antarctica and its definite recognition as a continent were the outcome of American energy and prescience. It is therefore the duty of the 120,000 members of the National Geographic Society to create a public sentiment that shall honor in our literature and in our history the achievements of Nathaniel B. Palmer and of Charles Wilkes.

FURTHER READING

An impressive history of Antarctica is G. E. Fogg and David Smith, The Exploration of Antarctica (1990). See also Roland Huntford, Scott and Amundsen (1980) and John Stewart, Antarctica: An Encyclopedia (1990). Diana Preston's A First Rate Tragedy: Robert Falcon Scott and the Race to the South Pole (1998), chronicles Scott's tragic attempt to be the first explorer to reach the South Pole.

An excellent book for younger readers is Sandra Markle's Super Cool Science: South Pole Stations, Past, Present, and Future (1998).

INDEX

CONTRIBUTORS

General Editor FRED L. ISRAEL is an award-winning historian. He received the Scribe's Award from the American Bar Association for his work on the Chelsea House series *The Justices of the United States Supreme Court*. A specialist in American history, he was general editor for Chelsea's *1897 Sears Roebuck Catalog*. Dr. Israel has also worked in association with Arthur M. Schlesinger, Jr. on many projects, including *The History of the U.S. Presidential Elections* and *The History of U.S. Political Parties*. He is senior consulting editor on the Chelsea House series *Looking into the Past: People, Places, and Customs*, which examines past traditions, customs, and cultures of various nations.

Senior Consulting Editor ARTHUR M. SCHLESINGER, JR. is the pre-eminent American historian of our time. He won the Pulitzer Prize for his book *The Age of Jackson* (1945), and again for *A Thousand Days* (1965). This chronicle of the Kennedy Administration also won a National Book Award. He has written many other books, including a multi-volume series, *The Age of Roosevelt*. Professor Schlesinger is the Albert Schweitzer Professor of the Humanities at the City University of New York, and has been involved in several other Chelsea House projects, including the *American Statesmen* series of biographies on the most prominent figures of early American history.